Our Human Rights

Book

ISSUES

Volume 167

Series Editor

Lisa Firth

Independence

Educational Publishers
Cambridge

First published by Independence
The Studio, High Green
Great Shelford
Cambridge CB22 5EG
England

© Independence 2009

British Library Cataloguing in Publication Data
Our Human Rights – (Issues Series)
I. Human rights II. Firth, Lisa
323

ISBN 978 1 86168 471 4

Printed in Great Britain
MWL Print Group Ltd

Cover
The illustration on the front cover is by
Simon Kneebone.

CONTENTS

Useful information for readers

Dear Reader,

Issues: Our Human Rights

Human rights are often the subject of controversy, with issues such as the Government's proposed 42 days' detention without charge for terror suspects making the news. In addition, there is divided public opinion about the UK's Human Rights Act and how it is being used. This book examines these issues, and also looks at topics which include torture, slavery, people trafficking, exploitation of children, child soldiers, terrorism, and whether smacking should or should not be considered an abuse of human rights.

The purpose of Issues

Our Human Rights is the one hundred and sixty-seventh volume in the **Issues** series. The aim of this series is to offer up-to-date information about important issues in our world. Whether you are a regular reader or new to the series, we do hope you find this book a useful overview of the many and complex issues involved in the topic. This title replaces an older volume in the **Issues** series, Volume 120: **The Human Rights Issue**, which is now out of print.

Titles in the **Issues** series are resource books designed to be of especial use to those undertaking project work or requiring an overview of facts, opinions and information on a particular subject, particularly as a prelude to undertaking their own research.

The information in this book is not from a single author, publication or organisation; the value of this unique series lies in the fact that it presents information from a wide variety of sources, including:

⇨ Government reports and statistics
⇨ Newspaper articles and features
⇨ Information from think-tanks and policy institutes
⇨ Magazine features and surveys
⇨ Website material
⇨ Literature from lobby groups and charitable organisations. *

Critical evaluation

Because the information reprinted here is from a number of different sources, readers should bear in mind the origin of the text and whether the source is likely to have a particular bias or agenda when presenting information (just as they would if undertaking their own research). It is hoped that, as you read about the many aspects of the issues explored in this book, you will critically evaluate the information presented. It is important that you decide whether you are being presented with facts or opinions. Does the writer give a biased or an unbiased report? If an opinion is being expressed, do you agree with the writer?

Our Human Rights offers a useful starting point for those who need convenient access to information about the many issues involved. However, it is only a starting point. Following each article is a URL to the relevant organisation's website, which you may wish to visit for further information.

Kind regards,

Lisa Firth
Editor, **Issues** series

Please note that Independence Publishers has no political affiliations or opinions on the topics covered in the Issues series, and any views quoted in this book are not necessarily those of the publisher or its staff.

Introducing human rights

Frequently asked questions

What are human rights?

Human rights belong to everyone. They are the basic rights we all have simply because we are human, regardless of who we are, where we live or what we do. Human rights allow us to flourish, reach our potential and participate fully in society. Human rights cover many aspects of everyday life ranging from the rights to food, shelter, education and health to freedoms of thought, religion and expression.

Human rights are underpinned by core values or principles, including fairness, respect, equality, dignity, autonomy, universality and participation. Human rights issues, values and principles are expressed through internationally agreed laws. These laws exist as a vehicle for making core human rights values real in people's lives.

'Human rights are not a privilege conferred by government. They are every human being's entitlement by virtue of his humanity.' Mother Teresa

Where do human rights come from?

The ideas behind human rights have been present throughout history in many different societies and civilisations. However, the modern concept of human rights emerged in the twentieth century as a response to the events of the Second World War, particularly the mass crimes committed during the Holocaust. States came together in 1948 at the United Nations to agree the 'Universal Declaration of Human Rights' (UDHR) – the most famous, most translated, and probably most important, human rights document.

The fundamental rights and freedoms outlined in the UDHR are expressed in international human rights treaties that are legally binding on states that agree to them, including the International Covenant on Civil and Political Rights and the International Covenant on Economic, Social and Cultural Rights. In total there are nine core UN human rights treaties.

The nine core UN human rights treaties are:

⇨ The International Covenant on Civil and Political Rights (ICCPR)
⇨ The International Covenant on Economic, Social and Cultural Rights (ICESCR)
⇨ The Convention Against Torture (CAT)
⇨ The Convention on the Elimination of Discrimination Against Women (CEDAW)
⇨ The Convention on the Elimination of Racial Discrimination (CERD)
⇨ The Convention on the Rights of the Child (CRC)
⇨ The International Convention on the Protection of the Rights of all Migrant Workers and Members of their Families (the UK has not signed this Convention)
⇨ The International Convention for the Protection of all Persons from Enforced Disappearances (not yet in force; the UK has not signed this Convention)
⇨ The Convention on the Rights of Persons with Disabilities (CRPD) (the UK has signed, but not yet ratified, this Convention).

Countries have also come together to agree regional human rights treaties such as the European Convention on Human Rights, the American Convention on Human Rights and the African Charter on Human and People's Rights. These treaties contain some, but not all, of the rights expressed in the UDHR.

Many countries also have their own domestic human rights laws – for example, in the UK we have the Human Rights Act. For more information on the different types of human rights laws, please see BIHR's 'Protecting human rights in the UK'.

'Human rights are inscribed in the hearts of the people; they were there long before lawmakers drafted their first proclamation.' Mary Robinson, Former United Nations High Commissioner for Human Rights

What kinds of rights are protected by human rights laws?

There are many human rights, which reflect different areas of our lives - spanning civil, political, economic, social, cultural and environmental aspects. All human rights are indivisible, interrelated and interdependent - restricting one right has a negative impact on other rights, while taking steps to fulfil a right facilitates the enjoyment of other rights. For example, restricting the right to health by not providing an adequate healthcare system may impact on other rights in a negative way such as the right to life. Enhancing the right to education through an effective education system for all can support the enjoyment of other rights such as the right to work.

Different human rights laws focus on different rights - for example there is an international treaty that covers civil and political rights (such as freedom of expression, and the right to liberty), and a separate international treaty encompassing economic, social and cultural rights (such as rights to education and health). Some international treaties focus on particular rights, such as the Convention against Torture. Other international treaties protect the rights of specific groups, for example women, children and disabled people. The existence of these treaties does not give these groups any additional rights, but recognises the particular discrimination and difficulties some groups face in claiming their human rights.

Can human rights ever be taken away or limited?

No one can have their human rights completely 'taken away' - even if they have not met their responsibilities or have compromised the rights of others. Some human rights are absolute, which means they can never be limited or restricted, in any circumstances - for example the right not to be tortured or treated in an inhuman or degrading way. However, the majority of human rights are not absolute and can be limited or restricted in certain circumstances. For example, if someone writes hate speech inciting murder against an ethnic group, their freedom of expression may be limited to ensure the safety of others. Social services may decide to remove a child from their home and place them in care if they have evidence that they are being abused by their parents, thus restricting the right to respect for family life. The conditions under which human rights can be restricted or limited are set out in the relevant human rights laws.

If human rights cannot be taken away, then how come there are so many human rights abuses happening in the world?

The fact that we all have human rights does not mean that they are always respected. It is evident that human rights abuses and violations continue to occur in different parts of the world, including in the UK. In order to make human rights a reality in all people's lives, it is essential that people know what their rights are and know how to claim them. It is equally vital that those responsible for protecting and respecting people's rights are aware of their obligations and are held to account for human rights abuses. Therefore, states and people within them must know what their rights are, what responsibilities they hold, and how these can be maintained, protected and fulfilled.

Who is responsible for upholding human rights?

The primary responsibility for upholding human rights lies with states. The human rights responsibilities of states are often broken down into obligations to respect, protect and fulfil rights.

⇨ The obligation to respect means that states must refrain from carrying out human rights abuses (for example not taking away someone's life arbitrarily, thus respecting the right to life).

⇨ The obligation to protect means that states must protect individuals and groups against human rights abuses by other actors (for example, protecting the right to life by making sure that life-sustaining medical treatment is not withdrawn unfairly).

Human rights belong to everyone. They are the basic rights we all have simply because we are human, regardless of who we are, where we live or what we do

---

⇨ The obligation to fulfil means that states must take positive steps to make human rights a reality in people's lives (for example improving the healthcare system, to ensure that lives are saved wherever possible - thus taking steps towards fulfilling the right to life).

Human rights provide minimum standards below which states cannot go, and also set goals for the constant improvement of these minimum standards.

Do individuals hold responsibilities to each other?

Human rights recognise that we all live alongside each other, and everyone else has rights too. This is why the majority of rights are non-absolute and can be limited or restricted in certain circumstances. If we compromise others' human rights, we are subject to laws that may limit our own rights as a result. For example, if we commit a crime we may be sent to jail, thus restricting our right to liberty. But more than this, human rights can be viewed as part of the relationships we have to each other and society as a whole, and therefore we have an ethical responsibility to respect each other's rights - even when in some instances those rights conflict with one's own. The state is ultimately accountable for balancing these sometimes conflicting rights.

Which human rights laws apply in the UK?

The main source of human rights law in the UK is the Human Rights Act, which came into force in 2000. The Human Rights Act incorporates most of the rights that are contained in the European Convention on Human Rights into UK law. The UK signed up to the European Convention in 1951. The UK has also signed all of the core international human rights treaties (see above), except for the Migrant Workers' Convention and the International Convention for the Protection of all Persons from Enforced Disappearances.

Why are human rights relevant to the UK?

Human rights belong to everyone in the UK and are relevant to many of the situations people experience and the decisions people make on a daily basis. The Human Rights Act provides a crucial safety net for protecting us all, particularly when we are facing disadvantage or discrimination, or are at our most vulnerable. The Human Rights Act also provides a useful framework for public authorities – including central and local government departments, hospitals, state schools and social services departments – within which decisions can be made and competing rights and interests can be balanced.

However, in the UK we tend to only hear about human rights being used by those who may have compromised other people's rights, such as criminals and terrorists. Although these groups still retain their core human rights, many of their rights will be restricted. But we rarely hear about how the Human Rights Act has been used, for example, to protect older people who are being abused in care homes, to ensure that disabled children are provided with transport to get to school and to protect women from domestic violence. There are many other examples of how the Human Rights Act has been used to improve the lives of people in the UK, both in and outside of the courtroom. Please see BIHR's report 'The Human Rights Act – Changing Lives' (2006) for just some examples.

'Where, after all, do universal human rights begin? In small places, close to home...' Eleanor Roosevelt

Human rights – changing lives in the UK

A disabled woman was told by her occupational therapy department that she needed a special ('profile') bed to allow carers to give her bed baths. She requested a double bed so that she could continue to sleep next to her husband. The local authority refused her request, even though she offered to pay the difference in cost between a single and a double bed. A stalemate ensued for 18 months until the woman was advised by the Disability Law Centre to invoke her right to respect for her private and family life under the Human Rights Act. Within three hours of putting this argument to the authority it found enough money to buy the double profile bed for her.

Where can I find more information or advice on human rights?

Please visit the Useful resources section of our website for more information about human rights. Liberty's 'Your Rights' website and the website of the Equality and Human Rights Commission are also useful sources of information on human rights in the UK. You can find out more about international human rights on the website for the UN High Commissioner for Human Rights, or on Amnesty International's website.

Please note that BIHR is unable to provide advice to individuals about human rights. Our website lists a range of organisations that provide advice. The Equality and Human Rights Commission has a helpline for discrimination and human rights issues and is a useful starting point for advice about human rights. Their helpline numbers are:

⇨ England: 0845 604 6610 (textphone: 0845 604 6620)
⇨ Wales: 0845 604 8810 (textphone: 0845 604 8820)
⇨ Scotland: 0845 604 5510 (textphone: 0845 604 5520)

⇨ The above information is reprinted with kind permission from the British Institute of Human Rights. Visit www.bihr.org.uk for more information.

© British Institute of Human Rights

Human rights and politics

A briefing from politics.co.uk

What are human rights?

Human rights are rights that are deemed to belong to all people as such – that is, by virtue of their humanity. In the past, rights so conceived have more commonly been known as natural rights or 'the rights of man'.

In this way, human rights are ascribed to all humanity, regardless of nationality or citizenship: the doctrine of human rights can therefore come into conflict with the doctrine of the sovereignty of governments and the law. This proclaimed 'universality' has historically led to the pursuit of the human rights agenda at the level of international co-operation in the postwar era.

In the UK today, a number of fundamental individual freedoms are protected by the Human Rights Act 1998. This requires all UK law to comply with the European Convention on Human Rights of 1950 (and its First and Sixth Protocols), makes the Convention enforceable in UK courts, and requires the judiciary to interpret domestic law so as to comply with the Convention. Appeals against the rulings of UK courts can still be taken to the European Court of Human Rights, as they could be prior to the Act.

The various Articles of the Convention proclaim the following: the right to life (Article 2); the prohibition of torture (Article 3); the prohibition of slavery and forced labour (Article 4); the right to liberty and security (Article 5); the right to a fair trial (Article 6); the prohibition of extra-legal punishment (Article 7); the right to respect for private and family life (Article 8); freedom of thought, conscience and religion (Article 9); freedom of expression (Article 10); freedom of assembly and association (Article 11); the right to marry (Article 12); the prohibition of discrimination (Article 14).

The First Protocol, moreover, proclaims the right to enjoyment of private property, the right to education and the right to free elections. The Sixth Protocol forbids the death penalty, except during times of war (and then only in line with the law).

Background

The modern, legal approach to human rights stems from the 1948 United Nations Declaration on Human Rights. This was the first international, secular agreement on the rights of man, which stemmed from the desire of the world's governments to prevent the recurrence of the atrocities of the Second World War by setting out a 'common standard of achievement for all peoples and all nations'.

The modern, legal approach to human rights stems from the 1948 United Nations Declaration on Human Rights. This was the first international, secular agreement on the rights of man

---

The text was, and remains, non-binding, but it retains its force as the primary authority on human rights, and has been supported by the UN's ongoing work to encourage its incorporation into domestic laws.

Shortly afterwards, in 1949, the Council of Europe was founded, to promote human rights, parliamentary democracy and the rule of law. Its principal instrument was to be the European Convention on Human Rights, published in 1950, which took up the rights proclaimed in the UN Declaration. The UK played a leading part in the drafting of the Convention, and was one of the first countries to ratify it, in 1951. Today, there are 46 parties to the Convention.

During the next ten years, an international judicial system of authority was established to ensure that participant states complied with the Convention. Under the system, the European Commission on Human Rights, set up in 1954, would examine complaints brought by individuals, organisations or other states and rule on their admissibility, before passing them to the Committee of Ministers of the Council of Europe. The Commission Committee of a contracting state then had three months in which to bring the case before the European Court of Human Rights (established in 1959) for a final, binding adjudication. Individuals were not permitted to bring cases to the Court until 1966.

The expansion of the Council of Europe in the 1980s and 1990s saw the workload of the Convention institutions grow dramatically, with the Commission handling 404 applications in 1981 and 4,750 in 1997, and the Court hearing 7 cases in 1981 and 119 in 1997. In 1998, the part-time Court was replaced with a full-time body.

The ECHR placed all of the original 1948 rights into three categories: absolute, limited and qualified. The prohibition of torture, as an absolute right, was not to be interfered with in any circumstances; limited rights, such as the right to liberty and security, could only be breached in line with the law of the land; and qualified rights could be interfered with if this was deemed to be 'necessary in a democratic society in the interests of public safety, for the protection of public order, health or morals, or the protection of the rights and freedoms of others'.

In 1997, the Labour government was elected pledging to incorporate the Convention directly into UK law. In the preceding years, a strong movement calling for this had built up in opposition to the ruling Conservative governments, which many opponents claimed had undermined the social and economic consensus that had prevailed until then - particularly in respect of labour rights. Lacking a codified constitution setting out the rights of citizens, many believed that the doctrine of Parliamentary Sovereignty did not provide adequate protections for individual rights from intrusive government. The subsequent Human Rights Act 1998 came into force on 2 October 2000.

Controversies

Human rights are controversial at the political and legal level because they proclaim the superiority of certain principles to nations' statute laws. The Human Rights Act 1998 resolved this conflict by explicitly bringing the Convention into UK law. However, although all other laws must comply with it, unlike many other nations' 'bills of rights', the HRA has no privileged position in UK law: unlike in the USA, where changes to the Constitution require special procedures, Parliament could repeal the HRA in the same way as any other law. It remains to be seen whether the 'Charter of Fundamental Rights' under consideration in the context of the draft EU Constitutional Treaty will alter this situation.

Also at the level of principle, there is considerable controversy as to what should be included amongst 'human' rights. Many have argued that 'economic rights' - such as those outlined in the First Protocol - are not basic natural rights in the same way as the right to life. Social conservatives have been outraged by legislation to recognise transgender people's new identities and to sanction homosexual partnerships, deemed by the Government as necessary under the HRA or the human rights agenda more widely.

Critics of the Act have also argued that it has undermined the authority of Parliament - and as such, democracy itself - by handing so much power to the judiciary. The Act permits judges to deem legislation to be incompatible, and while the Government can appeal these decisions, the ultimate ruling of the European Court is final. The Government, however, maintains that the balance has not shifted. While judges can issue 'declarations of incompatibility', they are not empowered to strike down incompatible laws: rather, the Government must decide how to respond to a declaration.

Nonetheless, there have been a number of high profile clashes between the Government and the courts over several criminal justice and immigration measures since the HRA came into force. Measures that have been challenged include the suspension of benefits for 'late claim' asylum seekers, the Home Secretary's power to set 'tariffs' on sentences and the detention of terrorist suspects without charge.

Human rights groups, on the other hand, argue that the Act does not go far enough, and point to numerous opportunities in the Convention for governments to opt out of certain provisions in the interests of national security. The widened definition of 'national security' in the post-September 11 world, it is argued, gives public authorities too much licence.

Statistics

Details of funding for human rights projects during 2000-2006 from the EIDHR (European Instrument for Democracy and Human Rights - a European programme which aims to support human rights and democracy worldwide) show that:

The three themes to receive the most funding were:
⇨ Promotion and Protection of Human Rights and Fundamental Freedoms - 156.8 million euros;
⇨ Torture - 75.5 million euros;
⇨ Governance - 73.0 million euros.

The three themes which attracted the most projects were:
⇨ Promotion and Protection of Human Rights and Fundamental Freedoms - 466 projects;
⇨ Governance - 345 projects;
⇨ Women - 184 projects.

The region receiving most EIDHR funding was Sub-Saharan Africa with 162, 959,801 million euros, followed by Latin America with 136,454,860 million euros.

North America and Europe received the least with 1,306,451 and 5,668,837 million euros respectively.
Source: EIDHR - 2008

Quotes

'We will not enjoy security without development, we will not enjoy development without security, and we will not enjoy either without respect for human rights.'
Former UN Secretary-General Kofi Annan

'The European Union believes that democracy and human rights are universal values that should be vigorously promoted around the world. They are integral to effective work on poverty alleviation and conflict prevention and resolution, in addition to being valuable bulwarks against terrorism.'
European Commission - 2008

⇨ The above information is reprinted with kind permission from politics.co.uk. Visit www.politics.co.uk for more information.

© Adfero

Human rights timeline

Some key developments

The modern concept of human rights has its foundations in the Universal Declaration of Human Rights, adopted by the United Nations in the aftermath of the Second World War. However, the ideas behind human rights have been present throughout history in many different societies and civilisations. This timeline explores some of the roots and origins of human rights and how they have developed throughout history into the conception we have today.

Human rights have emerged out of a wide range of ideas, laws, movements and events, and we have only been able to include a selection in this timeline. We have focused in particular on legal and institutional developments relevant to the UK.

1760 BC In Babylon King Hammurabi draws up the 'Code of Hammurabi', an early legal document that promises to 'make justice reign in the kingdom ... and promote the good of the people'.

c.528-486 BC In India, Buddha preaches morality, reverence for life, non-violence and right conduct.

c.26-33 AD In Palestine, Jesus Christ preaches morality, tolerance, justice, forgiveness and love.

613-632 In Saudi Arabia, Prophet Muhammad teaches the principles of equality, justice and compassion revealed in the Qur'an.

1215 In England the Magna Carta is agreed, limiting the power of the king and giving free men the right to be judged by their peers.

1689 The English Parliament agrees the English Bill of Rights, curtailing the power of the monarch and including the right to be free from torture and to punishment without trial.

1789 In France, the National Assembly agrees the French Declaration of the Rights of Man and of the Citizen, which guarantees the rights to liberty, equality, property, security and resistance to oppression.

1791 The United States Congress agrees the US Bill of Rights, amending the US Constitution to include rights to trial by jury, freedom of expression, speech, belief and assembly.

1833 The British Parliament abolishes slavery in the British Empire through the Slavery Abolition Act.

1893 New Zealand gives women the vote – the first country in the world to do this.

1919 The International Labour Organisation (ILO) is established to advocate for rights in labour law, e.g. employment discrimination and forced labour.

1934 The National Council for Civil Liberties (usually known as 'Liberty') is established, a non-governmental organisation that seeks to protect civil liberties and promote human rights for everyone in England and Wales.

1945 The United Nations (UN) is created 'to reaffirm faith in human rights, in the dignity and worth of the human person...'

1948 The Universal Declaration of Human Rights is adopted by the UN.

1950 The European Convention on Human Rights is adopted by the Council of Europe. The UK signed up to the Convention in 1951.

1961 Amnesty International is created by British lawyer Peter Benenson.

1964 The Civil Rights Bill is passed in the US, banning discrimination in voting, jobs, public accommodation and other activities.

1965 The International Convention on the Elimination of all Forms of Racial Discrimination is adopted and opened for signature by the UN – the first core human rights treaty to enter into force (in 1969).

1966 The International Covenant on Civil and Political Rights and the International Covenant on Economic, Social and Cultural Rights are adopted and opened for signature by the UN. They entered into force in 1976.

1968 The first world conference on human rights is held in Tehran.

1969 The American Convention on Human Rights is adopted by a large number of the nations of the Americas, entering into force in 1979.

1979 The Convention on the Elimination of Discrimination Against Women (CEDAW) is adopted and opened for signature by the UN. CEDAW entered into force in 1981.

1981 The African Charter on Human and Peoples' Rights is adopted by the Organisation of African Unity (now the African Union).

1984 The Convention Against Torture is adopted and opened for signature by the UN, entering into force in 1987.

1989 The Convention on the Rights of the Child is adopted and opened for signature by the UN, entering into force in 1990. This is the most widely ratified human rights treaty; only the USA and Somalia have not ratified the CRC.

1990 The Convention for the Protection of all Migrant Workers and Members of their Families is adopted and opened for signature by the UN. The UK has not signed up to this Convention.

1990 In South Africa, President F.W. de Klerk lifts the ban on the African National Congress (ANC) and other anti-apartheid organisations. Nelson Mandela is released from Robben Island Prison after 27 years of imprisonment.

1998 The Human Rights Act 1998 is adopted by the UK Parliament, making most of the rights contained in the European Convention on Human Rights part of UK law. The Act entered into force on 2 October 2000.

1999 The Northern Ireland Human Rights Commission is set up to promote awareness of the importance of human rights in Northern Ireland.

2007 The Convention on the Rights of Persons with Disabilities is adopted and opened for signature by the UN. The Convention received the highest number of signatories in history to a UN Convention on its opening day, and came into force in May 2008.

2007 The leaders of the 10 Association of Southeast Asian Nations (ASEAN) countries sign the first-ever ASEAN Charter, which contains a provision for the establishment of an ASEAN human rights body.

2007 The Government publishes the 'Governance of Britain' Green Paper, a set of wide-reaching proposals that look at how we should uphold and enhance the rights and responsibilities of the citizen.

2007 The Equality and Human Rights Commission is launched in Great Britain. The Commission works to eliminate discrimination, reduce inequality, promote human rights and build good relations throughout England, Scotland and Wales.
To be continued...

⇨ The above information is reprinted with kind permission from the British Institute of Human Rights. Visit www.bihr.org.uk for more information.

© British Institute of Human Rights

Public opinion on human rights

For 50 years Britain has been a member of the European Convention on Human Rights. This bans torture, and also prevents the deportation of anyone to any country where there is a significant risk of torture. As a result, convicted terrorists are able to remain in Britain after they have completed their prison sentences. Do you support or oppose the following proposal?

Britain should give a public warning that it has ceased to be a member of the Convention. It would then have the right to deport terrorists convicted after such a warning (on completion of their sentences), and without further appeal, even if this means sending them to countries where they might be tortured.

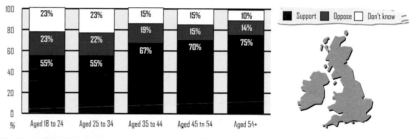

The Human Rights Convention also requires suspects to be treated the same, regardless of whether they have British or foreign nationality. Do you support or oppose the following proposals?

Britain should have, and use, the right to deport foreigners suspected by the intelligence services, even if there is not enough court room evidence to bring them to trial, and they might be sent to countries where they could be tortured.

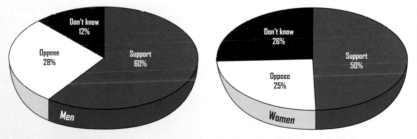

Britain should have, and use, the right to imprison foreign terrorist suspects for as long as the authorities judge necessary, unless they choose to return to their home country.

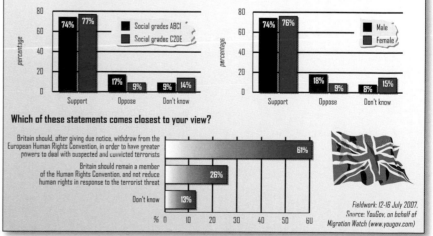

Which of these statements comes closest to your view?

Fieldwork: 12-16 July 2007. Source: YouGov, on behalf of Migration Watch (www.yougov.com)

The Universal Declaration of Human Rights

Adopted and proclaimed by General Assembly resolution 217 A (III) of 10 December 1948

All human beings are born with equal and inalienable rights and fundamental freedoms. The United Nations is committed to upholding, promoting and protecting the human rights of every individual. This commitment stems from the United Nations Charter, which reaffirms the faith of the peoples of the world in fundamental human rights and in the dignity and worth of the human person.

In the Universal Declaration of Human Rights, the United Nations has stated in clear and simple terms the rights which belong equally to every person.

These rights belong to you.

They are your rights. Familiarise yourself with them. Help to promote and defend them for yourself as well as for your fellow human beings.

Preamble

Whereas recognition of the inherent dignity and of the equal and inalienable rights of all members of the human family is the foundation of freedom, justice and peace in the world,

Whereas disregard and contempt for human rights have resulted in barbarous acts which have outraged the conscience of mankind, and the advent of a world in which human beings shall enjoy freedom of speech and belief and freedom from fear and want has been proclaimed as the highest aspiration of the common people,

Whereas it is essential, if man is not to be compelled to have recourse, as a last resort, to rebellion against tyranny and oppression, that human rights should be protected by the rule of law,

Whereas it is essential to promote the development of friendly relations between nations,

Whereas the peoples of the United Nations have in the Charter reaffirmed their faith in fundamental human rights, in the dignity and worth of the human person and in the equal rights of men and women and have determined to promote social progress and better standards of life in larger freedom,

Whereas Member States have pledged themselves to achieve, in co-operation with the United Nations, the promotion of universal respect for and observance of human rights and fundamental freedoms,

Whereas a common understanding of these rights and freedoms is of the greatest importance for the full realisation of this pledge,

Now, therefore, the General Assembly proclaims this Universal Declaration of Human Rights as a common standard of achievement for all peoples and all nations, to the end that every individual and every organ of society, keeping this Declaration constantly in mind, shall strive by teaching and education to promote respect for these rights and freedoms and by progressive measures, national and international, to secure their universal and effective recognition and observance, both among the peoples of Member States themselves and among the peoples of territories under their jurisdiction.

Article 1

All human beings are born free and equal in dignity and rights. They are endowed with reason and conscience and should act towards one another in a spirit of brotherhood.

Article 2

Everyone is entitled to all the rights and freedoms set forth in this Declaration, without distinction of any kind, such as race, colour, sex, language, religion, political or other opinion, national or social origin, property, birth or other status. Furthermore, no distinction shall be made on the basis of the political, jurisdictional or international status of the country or territory to which a person belongs, whether it be independent, trust, non-self-governing or under any other limitation of sovereignty.

Article 3
Everyone has the right to life, liberty and security of person.

Article 4
No one shall be held in slavery or servitude; slavery and the slave trade shall be prohibited in all their forms.

Article 5
No one shall be subjected to torture or to cruel, inhuman or degrading treatment or punishment.

Article 6
Everyone has the right to recognition everywhere as a person before the law.

Article 7
All are equal before the law and are entitled without any discrimination to equal protection of the law. All are entitled to equal protection against any discrimination in violation of this Declaration and against any incitement to such discrimination.

Article 8
Everyone has the right to an effective remedy by the competent national tribunals for acts violating the fundamental rights granted him by the constitution or by law.

Article 9
No one shall be subjected to arbitrary arrest, detention or exile.

Article 10
Everyone is entitled in full equality to a fair and public hearing by an independent and impartial tribunal, in the determination of his rights and obligations and of any criminal charge against him.

Article 11
(1) Everyone charged with a penal offence has the right to be presumed innocent until proved guilty according to law in a public trial at which he has had all the guarantees necessary for his defence.
(2) No one shall be held guilty of any penal offence on account of any act or omission which did not constitute a penal offence, under national or international law, at the time when it was committed. Nor shall a heavier penalty be imposed than the one that was applicable at the time the penal offence was committed.

Article 12
No one shall be subjected to arbitrary interference with his privacy, family, home or correspondence, nor to attacks upon his honour and reputation. Everyone has the right to the protection of the law against such interference or attacks.

All human beings are born with equal and inalienable rights and fundamental freedoms

---

Article 13
(1) Everyone has the right to freedom of movement and residence within the borders of each State.
(2) Everyone has the right to leave any country, including his own, and to return to his country.

Article 14
(1) Everyone has the right to seek and to enjoy in other countries asylum from persecution.
(2) This right may not be invoked in the case of prosecutions genuinely arising from non-political crimes or from acts contrary to the purposes and principles of the United Nations.

Article 15
(1) Everyone has the right to a nationality.
(2) No one shall be arbitrarily deprived of his nationality nor denied the right to change his nationality.

Article 16
(1) Men and women of full age, without any limitation due to race, nationality or religion, have the right to marry and to found a family. They are entitled to equal rights as to marriage, during marriage and at its dissolution.
(2) Marriage shall be entered into only with the free and full consent of the intending spouses.

(3) The family is the natural and fundamental group unit of society and is entitled to protection by society and the State.

Article 17
(1) Everyone has the right to own property alone as well as in association with others.
(2) No one shall be arbitrarily deprived of his property.

Article 18
Everyone has the right to freedom of thought, conscience and religion; this right includes freedom to change his religion or belief, and freedom, either alone or in community with others and in public or private, to manifest his religion or belief in teaching, practice, worship and observance.

Article 19 of the Universal Declaration of Human Rights enshrines the right to freedom of opinion and expression

Article 19
Everyone has the right to freedom of opinion and expression; this right includes freedom to hold opinions without interference and to seek, receive and impart information and ideas through any media and regardless of frontiers.

Article 20
(1) Everyone has the right to freedom of peaceful assembly and association.
(2) No one may be compelled to belong to an association.

Article 21
(1) Everyone has the right to take part in the government of his country, directly or through freely chosen representatives.
(2) Everyone has the right of equal access to public service in his country.

(3) The will of the people shall be the basis of the authority of government; this will shall be expressed in periodic and genuine elections which shall be by universal and equal suffrage and shall be held by secret vote or by equivalent free voting procedures.

Article 22

Everyone, as a member of society, has the right to social security and is entitled to realisation, through national effort and international co-operation and in accordance with the organisation and resources of each State, of the economic, social and cultural rights indispensable for his dignity and the free development of his personality.

Article 23

(1) Everyone has the right to work, to free choice of employment, to just and favourable conditions of work and to protection against unemployment.
(2) Everyone, without any discrimination, has the right to equal pay for equal work.
(3) Everyone who works has the right to just and favourable remuneration ensuring for himself and his family an existence worthy of human dignity, and supplemented, if necessary, by other means of social protection.
(4) Everyone has the right to form and to join trade unions for the protection of his interests.

Article 24

Everyone has the right to rest and leisure, including reasonable limitation of working hours and periodic holidays with pay.

Article 25

(1) Everyone has the right to a standard of living adequate for the health and well-being of himself and of his family, including food, clothing, housing and medical care and necessary social services, and the right to security in the event of unemployment, sickness, disability, widowhood, old age or other lack of livelihood in circumstances beyond his control.
(2) Motherhood and childhood are entitled to special care and assistance. All children, whether born in or out of wedlock, shall enjoy the same social protection.

Article 26

(1) Everyone has the right to education. Education shall be free, at least in the elementary and fundamental stages. Elementary education shall be compulsory. Technical and professional education shall be made generally available and higher education shall be equally accessible to all on the basis of merit.
(2) Education shall be directed to the full development of the human personality and to the strengthening of respect for human rights and fundamental freedoms. It shall promote understanding, tolerance and friendship among all nations, racial or religious groups, and shall further the activities of the United Nations for the maintenance of peace.
(3) Parents have a prior right to choose the kind of education that shall be given to their children.

Article 27

(1) Everyone has the right freely to participate in the cultural life of the community, to enjoy the arts and to share in scientific advancement and its benefits.
(2) Everyone has the right to the protection of the moral and material interests resulting from any scientific, literary or artistic production of which he is the author.

Article 28

Everyone is entitled to a social and international order in which the rights and freedoms set forth in this Declaration can be fully realised.

Article 29

(1) Everyone has duties to the community in which alone the free and full development of his personality is possible.
(2) In the exercise of his rights and freedoms, everyone shall be subject only to such limitations as are determined by law solely for the purpose of securing due recognition and respect for the rights and freedoms of others and of meeting the just requirements of morality, public order and the general welfare in a democratic society.
(3) These rights and freedoms may in no case be exercised contrary to the purposes and principles of the United Nations.

Article 30

Nothing in this Declaration may be interpreted as implying for any State, group or person any right to engage in any activity or to perform any act aimed at the destruction of any of the rights and freedoms set forth herein.

⇨ The above information is a public information document meant to inform about the Universal Declaration of Human Rights during its 60th anniversary. Visit www.un.org for more information.

© *Public domain*

Tears and smiles in the fight for justice

Sixty years ago, in the wake of the Holocaust, the UN issued its Universal Declaration of Human Rights proclaiming 'the basic rights and freedoms to which all humans are entitled'. Here, we talk to five people fighting for human rights.

Marjorie Nshemere Ojule

32, Ugandan refugee, now a trustee of Women for Refugee Women in the UK

'If my husband is out there, if he sees my photo, I would love him to contact me'

In Uganda I was active in opposition politics at a grassroots level: working in my village, helping women to know their rights and teaching them reading and writing. I was detained twice. The horror that I experienced in there, you wouldn't wish that on anyone, not even your enemy. I was tortured, I was raped, I was burnt with cigarettes, I was cut with razors, electric shocks: all the horrible things you can think of to get information from someone. Eventually I escaped and came to England. It was scary but I'd been in this torture for some time, and I just wanted to be able to breathe fresh air again. I left my husband when I escaped and that's the last time I saw him. I don't have a clue where he is. If he's out there, if he sees my photo, I would love him to contact me. I may be dreaming about him when he's already dead but life is full of surprises.

The child I have now is out of rape and at first I didn't want to keep her, I wanted to put her up for adoption. When I arrived in 2002, they took me to the hospital: I was malnourished, I was dehydrated, I didn't have any blood and the Home Office told me I had to go home when the child was born. After six months they wanted to check my daughter was healthy and it was only after that they said 'Oh by the way we have a family for her'. I said I'm not ready to give someone my child if they first want to see if

Interviews by Hermione Hoby, Hugh Montgomery, Tom Parfitt and Sibylla Brodzinsky

she's developing at the normal rate and so on. At this time I was going to counselling and it made me a strong person: my wounds had healed, I was looking and feeling myself and I realised this child was part of me. It's difficult bringing her up but if I didn't have her I would have gone insane waiting for a decision from the Home Office.

It's easy to say, 'Oh asylum seekers have taken all the houses and so on', but the truth is that asylum seekers really suffer in the current system. When my case was heard in court, the judge agreed that I was tortured and gave me leave to remain on human-rights grounds. But the Home Office appealed against that decision. That was in 2004 and, until January this year, I was living in limbo, waiting to hear the outcome. Finally they gave me indefinite leave to remain.

I got tired of sitting at home so I started looking for charities and it was through Women for Refugee Women

that I met Natasha [Walter, who runs the charity]. I've been public speaking ever since, telling my story and telling the stories of other women who can't speak English. It felt like therapy as well: when there's a place where you can explode with anger and say 'why would the government do this?' it feels good afterwards, like I could breathe properly. Everyone asks me, 'Oh my God, Marjorie, how did you manage to deal with all these things?' I'd say the work I do with you keeps me busy. I've been to the House of Commons I don't know how many times. The first time was so scary but when I stood up and spoke, I looked around and everyone was nodding and I thought: oh my God, I have power. You can make me sign [for asylum seekers' financial support] 1,001 times a day [asylum seekers have to sign regularly to comply with Home Office regulations. Breach of signing requirements can result in detention] but you can't take my brains out of my head. I thought 'Way to go, woman!' Natasha tells me I'm amazing and I say, 'I'm amazing because of you'. That makes me cry because if it wasn't for people like that I could not have had that power. I am so grateful to them.

I'm putting in an application for my 10-year-old daughter to come here because my mother, her guardian, passed away. Looking forward to meeting her – that hope keeps me going.
refugeewomen.com

Hollman Morris

40, Colombian journalist, winner of the 2007 Human Rights Watch Human Rights Defender Award

'I had to find out how people were slaughtered and nothing happened'

My seven-year-old daughter asked me a while ago, 'Daddy, why do you only interview sad people?' She had just seen one of my shows where I talked to victims of Colombia's conflict but I explained to her they are not just sad, they also have dreams, hope and dignity...

The people I interview are the voice of the 'other' Colombia, a Colombia that you don't see in most media, a Colombia that some people wish didn't exist. I knew from when I set out to be a journalist that my job was to show their stories.

I first saw that need when I was a teenager watching the TV news and when they reported about a massacre in Segovia where 70 people were killed in one day (11 November 1988) and I thought 'Shit, what is that about?' and then a few hours later we were watching a national beauty contest. That defined my role as a journalist because I decided I had to find out how it could be in this country that people were being slaughtered and nothing happened.

That has always meant problems for me with all the armed actors in the Colombian conflict. Since 1997 there have always been death threats from one group or another. But the most critical year of my life was between 2000 and 2001. A colleague who had been kidnapped and raped (by paramilitaries) said her captors had told her: 'Hollman Morris is next.' Around the same time my wife Patty told me she was pregnant. We fled to Spain with the help of an Amnesty International programme for human rights defenders because I was able to show my work from a human rights perspective.

After a year we came back to Colombia. My options for work in Spain were to do menial tasks, be a parking lot attendant. So it was a choice between shooting myself [out of frustration] in Spain or I get shot doing what I love in Colombia.

Our job as journalists is to look after people's rights. In a way we are

the guardians of human rights. We may not be the activists who put out urgent action notices every day. But our work as journalists is to write, publish and denounce when there is a violation of any fundamental right.

My generation has never seen a day of peace in Colombia. What I want is through journalism to try to build a better country for my children to live in so that they can live in peace.

Zmitser Dashkevich

27, leader of Youth Front, Belarus

'I received hundreds of letters of support every day from all over the world'

I was arrested in September 2006 and charged with 'organising and participating in the activity of an unregistered non-governmental organisation'. After six weeks in detention and on trial I was sentenced to one-and-a-half years in prison.

At that time I was leader of Youth Front, which is a Christian organisation of young people in Belarus. It is an independent political and social force which is in stark opposition to President Alexander Lukashenko, the last dictator in Europe. Lukashenko has openly praised Stalin and wants to turn our country back into the evil empire, the Soviet Union. We believe his politics are leading to the spiritual and moral degeneration of Belarusian society.

On six occasions we have tried to register our organisation but every time our application was refused. In early 2006 Lukashenko became very worried in the run-up to presidential elections. He understood that he was losing his power because the younger generation – despite all the ideology and repression – did not support him. Young people are mostly pro-European and pro-democratic in outlook. We were holding protests against falsification of the vote. So he introduced a new article into the law making it illegal to participate in the activities of an unregistered organisation. I was the first to be prosecuted.

After sentencing I was sent to prison. We slept in barracks and ate porridge and rotten meat. Very soon I started receiving hundreds of letters of support every day. They came from ordinary Belarusians, from Christian organisations and from members of human-rights groups from all over the world. These activists also sent thousands of letters to the government. And they sent lots of origami cranes – a symbol of freedom. I received some in prison. The censors checked my post and they unfolded the cranes to see if anything was inside. So I just received these creased, flattened-out pieces of coloured paper. But it was a powerful statement.

The government had painted us oppositionists as a sad, marginal group on the payroll of the CIA. But when the prison guards saw all my letters, they said: 'Wow, the people are really behind this guy.' They started to understand the gap between the propaganda and reality. Even the administrators admitted the letters were proof of something big. It altered their outlook. As a direct result of the huge campaign of public solidarity I was released one-and-a-half months early and returned to lead Youth Front. We are still struggling against Lukashenko's regime but now they are too afraid to imprison people under the registration law.

Odette Mupenzi

31, victim of Rwandan genocide
'I was very ill... I wanted to commit suicide. Now, I feel alive again'

I realised being a Tutsi was not considered good by some people when I was 11, because I had a teacher who picked on us, saying we had funny faces. Then in 1990 [the majority Hutus] killed many Tutsi intellectuals in a stadium near where I lived. After that, I knew we were in danger, but I didn't expect what was coming.

In January 1994, my family stopped sleeping at home because we thought we would be taken away during the night. When the genocide began in April, we fled to a religious seminary. The next day, lots of people turned up with machetes, guns, spears and axes.

Many of us hid in a classroom. They came to the door and my father opened it, because they threatened to burn the building down. When he did, I saw them cut him open. I was hiding under a mattress and they put a gun to my face and shot me. I could hear people praying, then there was silence – everyone was dead. The next thing I remember was waking up in hospital.

I've been fighting for life ever since. In Rwanda, all they did was wash the wound. An NGO helped me get treatment in Switzerland, but they ran out of money. I went to Germany and the same thing happened.

I first met the human-rights group Aegis Trust when it set up a genocide memorial in Kigali [in 2004]. I was very ill at the time - my bones were infected and I was living on morphine.

In March 2006, I came to England. I've had metal bones put in my jaw, and skin taken from my side and put in my face. I don't think people at home would recognise me. I can eat with a spoon and fork and drink from a tap. I don't know how to explain how the trust has helped me - thank you isn't enough. When they met me, I wanted to commit suicide. Now, I feel alive again.

To be honest, I don't want to go back to Rwanda. The war has stopped, but there are still troubles – survivors have been killed to stop them testifying against people. I just want to live in a country where I don't have to look over my shoulder all the time.

aegistrust.org

Ignatius Mahendra Kusuma Wardhana

25, Indonesian student activist
'They put me in a cell. There were a lot of blood prints over the walls'

I was imprisoned when I was 20 due to my involvement in the National Student League for Democracy. In January 2003, the President brought in a new policy to increase fuel and electricity prices, so mass demonstrations took place across Indonesia. We held a demonstration in Jakarta and it ended with a performance in which we burnt pictures of the President and Vice President. The police surrounded us and one of my friends was captured. I was not arrested at this point because the police didn't have a warrant. But my friend was blindfolded and they threatened him, saying they would shoot him and throw his body in the sea. He told me all this afterwards - at the time we didn't realise that he was captured.

When we went to the police station to find him, they gave me the warrant and arrested me. They interrogated me for about seven hours and a lot of the questions were not about the demonstration but about my organisation, who I was dealing with and so on. They put me in a cell that they called 'the tiger cage' because there was no bathroom in there; it's like when you're in the zoo and you see animals in a cage. It's a place where the police beat up prisoners too so there were a lot of blood prints over the walls.

In every trial the President's supporter came and threatened me and my lawyer. Maybe my lawyer was not brave enough because at the sixth or seventh trial he backed down and gave up. I was in despair because I thought I had no other way out. In April 2003 I was sentenced to three years. I was put in a cell they called the dry cell because there is no water at all - they gave us a drink once a day. There was a prisoner who sort of ran the prison, a member of the President's party, who fought me every week. Well, it wasn't really a fight because they were about 20 people and I am only one. The prison officer knew what was going on but I guess he was given money.

Amnesty International is familiar with the Indonesian movement and it made a greeting-card campaign, sending cards to me and to the Indonesian President. I counted more than 4,000 letters. They made me feel better and gave me hope but, most important, they meant that the prison officer was more careful with me. I was there for two years, seven months and three days: I counted every day but the most significant factor in keeping my spirits up was the campaign. When I got letters from children in the UK I just couldn't believe that they were aware of me and were doing something about it.

Indonesia is in a transitional period right now and there is still a lot to do for human rights. The first thing I did when I was released was demonstrate outside the prison because even though we got a new President with the 2004 election, he has continued repressive policies against activists. Prison is a bad memory but I got a lot of experience and lessons from it. I'm going to study human rights and politics at York University in October and after that I will continue my organisation. This is what I live for, this struggle.

⇨ This article first appeared in *The Observer*, 21 September 2008
© *Guardian Newspapers Limited 2008*

Amnesty International Report 2008

Facts and figures

Article 1

1948 Promise: All human beings are born free and equal in dignity and rights.

2008 Reality: In the first half of 2007 nearly 250 women were killed by violent husbands or family members in Egypt and on average 2 women were raped there every hour.

Article 3

1948 Promise: Everyone has the right to life, liberty and security of person.

2008 Reality: 1,252 people were known to have been executed by their state in 2007 in 24 countries; 104 countries, however, voted for a global moratorium on the death penalty.

Article 5

1948 Promise: No one shall be subjected to torture or to cruel, inhuman or degrading treatment or punishment.

2008 Reality: Amnesty International documented cases of torture and other cruel, inhuman or degrading treatment in more than 81 countries in 2007.

Article 7

1948 Promise: All are equal before the law and are entitled without any discrimination to equal protection of the law.

2008 Reality: Amnesty International's report highlights at least 23 countries with laws discriminating against women, at least 15 with laws discriminating against migrants and at least 14 with laws discriminating against minorities.

Article 9

1948 Promise: No one shall be subjected to arbitrary arrest, detention or exile.

2008 Reality: At the end of 2007, there were more than 600 people detained without charge, trial or judicial review of their detentions at the US airbase in Bagram, Afghanistan, and 25,000 held by the Multinational Force in Iraq.

Article 10

1948 Promise: Everyone charged with a crime is entitled equally to a fair and public hearing by an independent and impartial tribunal.

2008 Reality: 54 countries were recorded in the Amnesty International Report 2008 as conducting unfair trials.

Article 11

1948 Promise: Everyone has the right to be presumed innocent until proved guilty according to law.

2008 Reality: Amnesty International figures show that around 800 people have been held at Guantánamo Bay since the detention facility opened in January 2002, some 270 are still being held there in 2008 without charge or due legal process.

Article 13

1948 Promise: Everyone has the right to freedom of movement and residence within the borders of each state.

2008 Reality: In 2007, there were more than 550 Israeli military checkpoints and blockades restricting or preventing the movement of Palestinians between towns and villages in the West Bank.

Article 18

1948 Promise: Everyone has the right to freedom of thought, conscience and religion.

2008 Reality: Amnesty International has documented 45 countries as detaining Prisoners of Conscience.

Article 19

1948 Promise: Everyone has the right to freedom of opinion and expression, and to seek, receive and impart information and ideas through any media and regardless of frontiers.

2008 Reality: 77 countries were restricting freedom of expression and the press according to the Amnesty International Report 2008.

Article 20

1948 Promise: Everyone has the right to freedom of peaceful assembly and association.

2008 Reality: Thousands of people are believed to have been arrested during the crackdown on protests in Myanmar in 2007, Amnesty International estimates that around 700 remain in detention.

Article 23

1948 Promise: Everyone has the right to work, to free choice of employment, to fair and equal pay, and to form and join trade unions.

2008 Reality: At least 39 trade unionists were killed in Colombia in 2007, 22 have died in the first 4 months of this year.

Article 25

1948 Promise: Everyone has the right to a standard of living adequate for their health and well-being, especially mothers and children.

2008 Reality: 14% of Malawi's population was living with HIV/AIDS in 2007, only 3% of them had access to free anti-retroviral drugs, 1 million children were orphaned there by HIV/AIDS-related deaths.

All figures from Amnesty International Report 2008.

⇨ The above information is reprinted with kind permission from Amnesty International. Visit www.amnesty.org for more information.

Inside the Human Rights Act

Information from Liberty

What is the Human Rights Act?

The Human Rights Act is a written law (statute) passed in 1998 which is in force in England and Wales. The human rights that are contained within this law are based on the articles of the European Convention on Human Rights. That is why, when we talk about the rights granted by the Human Rights Act we often refer to them as 'Convention rights'.

Who can use it?

The Human Rights Act may be used by every person resident in England or Wales regardless of whether or not they are a British citizen or a foreign national, a child or an adult, a prisoner or a member of the public. It can even be used by companies or organisations (like Liberty).

What does it actually do?

The Act 'gives further effect' to rights and freedoms guaranteed under the European Convention on Human Rights. What this actually means is that it does two things:

⇨ Judges must read and give effect to legislation (other laws) in a way which is compatible with the Convention rights.

⇨ It is unlawful for a public authority to act in a way which is incompatible with a Convention right.

What rights does it protect?

The right to life – protects your life, by law. The state is required to investigate suspicious deaths and deaths in custody.

The prohibition of torture and inhuman treatment – you should never be tortured or treated in an inhuman or degrading way, no matter what the situation.

Protection against slavery and forced labour – you should not be treated like a slave or subjected to forced labour.

The right to liberty and freedom – you have the right to be free and the state can only imprison you with very good reason – for example, if you are convicted of a crime.

The right to a fair trial and no punishment without law – you are innocent until proven guilty. If accused of a crime, you have the right to hear the evidence against you, in a court of law.

Respect for privacy and family life and the right to marry – protects against unnecessary surveillance or intrusion into your life. You have the right to marry and raise a family.

Freedom of thought, religion and belief – you can believe what you like and practise your religion or beliefs.

Free speech and peaceful protest – you have a right to speak freely and join with others peacefully, to express your views.

No discrimination – everyone's rights are equal. You should not be treated unfairly – because, for example, of your gender, race, sexuality, religion or age.

Protection of property, the right to an education and the right to free elections – protects against state interference with your possessions; means that no child can be denied an education and that elections must be free and fair.

What does that mean for me?

Well, if you can show that a public authority has interfered with any of the rights recognised by the Convention you can take action in a number of different ways. For example:

⇨ You could simply write to the public authority concerned and remind them of their legal obligations under the Human Rights Act and ask them to rectify the situation.

⇨ If you went to court the court may find that a particular action (or inaction) of a public authority is (or would be) unlawful. It can tell the public authority to stop interfering with your right or to take action to protect your right.

⇨ If the court is satisfied that a provision of a law is incompatible with a Convention right, it may make a declaration of that incompatibility. This is just a formal legal statement that the particular law interferes with human rights. It does not have immediate effect but strongly encourages Parliament to amend or repeal the law in question.

⇨ The above information is re-printed with kind permission from Liberty. Visit www.liberty-human-rights.org.uk for more information.

© Liberty

Human Rights Act is a law for ne'er-do-wells

By Philip Johnston

Promises hastily made in opposition are often repented at leisure in government. Today, exactly 10 years after the passage of the Human Rights Act through Parliament, ministers have not exactly put out the bunting in celebration, though its chief architect Jack Straw, now Lord Chancellor, recently delivered an anniversary encomium.

The Act was, he said, a 'defining piece of legislation, a landmark which set the liberties we have long enjoyed in the United Kingdom on to a constitutional footing'. He added: 'I believe that the 1998 Act will be seen as one of the great legal, constitutional and social reforms of this government.'

Mr Straw said that many of the concerns initially voiced about the HRA had proved unfounded. It had not clogged up the courts with vexatious litigation, nor had it 'thrown common sense out of the window'.

Really? The wheels of justice may not have ground to a halt but the Act has proved to be a nice little earner for members of the legal profession, cited in more than 4,000 cases since it came into force and with about 1,200 human rights lawyers now practising in Britain. And extra court expenditure is estimated at £100million.

This would, perhaps, be a small price to pay if it were really reinforcing 'human rights'. But the cases that inspired Labour to promise to introduce the Act tended to involve defeats for the British government in the Strasbourg court over issues such as deportation of suspected terrorists and the release of life prisoners.

The basic liberties whose denial led to the promulgation of the European Convention on Human Rights (ECHR) in 1948 – such as the right not to be rounded up because of your religion, and murdered – were already well established in this country. Indeed, we went to war to defend them.

Those who drew up the convention were concerned about fundamental freedoms; yet the circumstances in which it has been applied in the UK have often been a travesty of that original purpose, and certainly involved the defenestration of Mr Straw's idea of common sense.

> **The concept of rights, once a noble cause, has been devalued by its association with a culture of grievance and egocentricity**

Take a case with which he was intimately involved. In February 2000, when he was Home Secretary, a plane was hijacked in Afghanistan and flown to Stansted Airport at the point of several guns. After an armed siege, nine hijackers and many of their relatives on board were arrested.

In the Commons, Mr Straw said: 'As a matter of public policy, I believe that the clearest and most unequivocal signals must be sent out so as to discourage hijacking, whatever its motive... I am determined that nobody should consider that there can be any benefit to be obtained by hijacking.

'Subject to compliance with all legal requirements, I would wish to see removed from this country all those on the plane as soon as reasonably practicable.'

The key words in that sentence were 'subject to compliance with all legal requirements' because the ECHR, as incorporated into the Human Rights Act, turned Mr Straw's fine words into so much hot air.

The hijackers are still in the country and have been given leave to stay indefinitely, even though British troops helped topple the Taliban from whom they said they were fleeing.

The concern of many critics was that the HRA would mark a shift in power from Parliament to the judiciary, which has happened; and that common sense would be suppressed for fear of infringing rights. That has happened, too.

When the Bill was going through Parliament, Lord McCluskey, the Scottish judge and vice-chairman of the Human Rights Institute of the International Bar Association, said: 'By incorporating into our domestic law

vague, imprecise and high-sounding statements of legal rights, we hand what is truly legislative power away from a democratic and accountable Parliament to an appointed, unelected and unaccountable judiciary.'

This led to bizarre decisions such as the failure to eject foreign nationals deemed a threat to our security; but it also engendered a set of attitudes in the public sector, especially in the criminal justice system, that have erred too much on the side of caution for fear of litigation.

The most egregious example was exposed by the report into the rape and murder of Naomi Bryant in Winchester in 2005.

It found that her killer, Anthony Rice, who had previously been imprisoned for life for rape, had been freed on licence after the Parole Board allowed its public protection obligations to be undermined by human rights considerations.

Another pernicious impact has been the assumption by any ne'er-do-well that he can invoke human rights for every eventuality. The concept of rights, once a noble cause, has been devalued by its association with a culture of grievance and egocentricity.

This entrenchment of rights was meant to be balanced by an acceptance of responsibility. Can anyone say that this has been properly struck?

The most grotesque development in recent years has been the reduction in the liberties – especially the privacy – of the law-abiding citizen, whom the state feels quite justified in bugging, harassing, and snooping upon, while at the same time those who have broken the law, or who are suspected of doing the nation great harm, are protected by the full majesty of the Human Rights Act.

Ten years on, was that really what Mr Straw and his colleagues had in mind?

10 November 2008

© *Telegraph Group Ltd, London 2008*

Mythbuster: the Human Rights Act

Separating fact from fiction

What does the Human Rights Act do for me? It isn't for the ordinary man in the street.

The Human Rights Act protects everyone's human rights; young and old, rich and poor, yours and mine. Anybody's privacy could be breached by the prying eyes of the state, anybody can be wrongly accused of a crime, and anybody could fall foul of careless and insensitive decision-making by public authorities. Hopefully this won't happen to you but, if it did, you might find you need to rely on the Human Rights Act to help you.

Thankfully we don't live in a totalitarian state where torture is rife and the press are gagged but we should not take our basic rights and freedoms for granted.

The Human Rights Act doesn't protect the victims of crime – just terrorists and criminals.

Human rights law has actually played an important part in protecting the rights of victims. For example, it has given bereaved relatives the right to an independent public investigation into the circumstances surrounding the death of their loved ones and the right to be involved in the investigation.

Human rights laws don't give criminals an easy ride. The Act specifically says those suspected of or convicted of crimes can be deprived of their liberty. The Human Rights Act also requires serious offences like murder, terrorism and rape to be investigated by the police and requires the state to take practical steps to protect people whose rights are threatened by others.

Human rights laws might have been needed 60 years ago, after the horrors of the Second World War, but they now need to change to meet the requirements of the modern world. People now have a 'human right' to anything.

Human rights are just as important today as they were 60 years ago. The people who experienced the horrors of the Second World War realised that protecting everyone's human rights was the best way of making sure that such atrocities never happen again. Thankfully, countries like the UK that have remained committed to protecting human rights have not seen repeats of the horrors of the Second World War. Sadly, war and civil unrest is still rife in countries where human rights violations remain a tragic reality. We cannot call for an end to rights abuses elsewhere in the world unless we show a commitment to protecting rights at home as well.

The Human Rights Act doesn't protect an endless catalogue of rights. Indeed, it only protects 15 well-established fundamental rights and freedoms, like the right to life and free speech. Many other democracies protect a far broader range of rights. Our human rights laws do not, for example, create general rights to a home, to live in the UK or to receive benefits.

The horrors perpetrated during the Holocaust at concentration camps such as Auschwitz (pictured) prompted the creation of the Universal Declaration of Human Rights in 1948. But is it still relevant today?

The Human Rights Act has made us all less safe. It needs amending so that the courts are required to balance our rights to safety and security.

The Human Rights Act already requires the courts to balance human rights against the interests of public safety. For example, the Act allows the right to freedom, speech, protest and privacy to be restricted where this is necessary to protect public safety or national security. Human rights law also requires the state to protect our safety and security.

The Human Rights Act protects everyone's human rights; young and old, rich and poor, yours and mine

---

Why shouldn't we be able to deport foreigners who pose a threat to our national security?

In the vast majority of cases human rights law does not stop people who threaten our national security from being deported. It does stop us deporting people to countries where they will face torture because in civilised societies like ours, we abhor the use of such barbaric treatment.

In fact, even before the Human Rights Act, the law made it clear that countries that respect human rights should not deport people to face torture elsewhere in the world.

Deporting dangerous terrorists doesn't make security sense either. Surely, rather than exporting the risk from terrorism, we would be safer if we prosecuted dangerous terrorists in the UK and, if they are found guilty, put them behind bars?

The Human Rights Act has cost the British taxpayer millions of pounds and has been a goldmine for lawyers. It has taken power away from the people we elected and given it to the judges.

One of the main reasons for the Act was the cost and delay caused by the fact that people could only enforce their human rights by taking cases to a court in Strasbourg. People's rights can now be protected by British courts, which is far more efficient and cost-effective. But the Human Rights Act is not just about lawyers and courts. It has helped thousands of people protect their human rights without the need for costly court cases. Local authorities have reviewed their policies to make sure they treat the vulnerable with dignity and respect and users of a wide range of public services have used the Act as a tool to argue for better and fairer services.

Our elected politicians passed the Human Rights Act; it wasn't invented by the judges. Neither did the Act transfer huge law-making powers to the courts. Even if a judge thinks that a law made by Parliament breaches our human rights they cannot overturn it. Our MPs still have the final say. What the Act did was to give the courts the tools to protect our human rights against abuse by the Government and powerful public bodies.

The Human Rights Act has been imposed on us by Europe.

No one forced the Human Rights Act upon us, the British public voted for it. Before the 1997 general election the Labour Party promised that, if we voted for them, they would give people the power to enforce their human rights in UK courts. When they won by a landslide majority they delivered this promise by passing the Human Rights Act. Also the Act is based on the European Convention on Human Rights which has nothing to do with Brussels or the EU – in fact the British played a major role in drawing up the Convention which includes many rights and freedoms that we have enjoyed for centuries in this country.

⇨ The above information is re-printed with kind permission from Liberty. Visit www.liberty-human-rights.org.uk for more information.

© *Liberty*

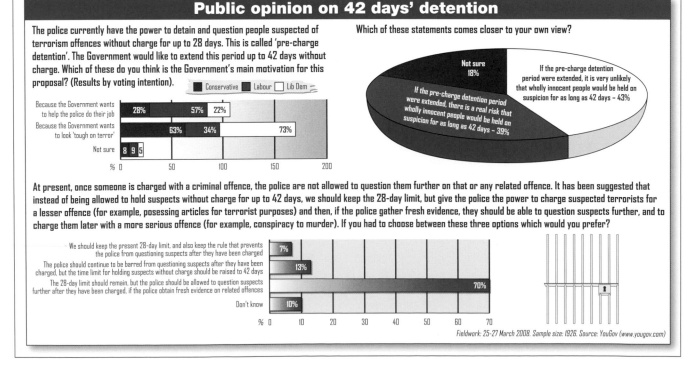

Public opinion on 42 days' detention

The police currently have the power to detain and question people suspected of terrorism offences without charge for up to 28 days. This is called 'pre-charge detention'. The Government would like to extend this period up to 42 days without charge. Which of these do you think is the Government's main motivation for this proposal? (Results by voting intention).

Conservative · Labour · Lib Dem

	Conservative	Labour	Lib Dem
Because the Government wants to help the police do their job	28%	57%	22%
Because the Government wants to look 'tough on terror'	63%	34%	73%
Not sure	8	9	5

% 0 · 50 · 100 · 150 · 200

Which of these statements comes closer to your own view?

- Not sure 18%
- If the pre-charge detention period were extended, it is very unlikely that wholly innocent people would be held on suspicion for as long as 42 days – 43%
- If the pre-charge detention period were extended, there is a real risk that wholly innocent people would be held on suspicion for as long as 42 days – 39%

At present, once someone is charged with a criminal offence, the police are not allowed to question them further on that or any related offence. It has been suggested that instead of being allowed to hold suspects without charge for up to 42 days, we should keep the 28-day limit, but give the police the power to charge suspected terrorists for a lesser offence (for example, posessing articles for terrorist purposes) and then, if the police gather fresh evidence, they should be able to question suspects further, and to charge them later with a more serious offence (for example, conspiracy to murder). If you had to choose between these three options which would you prefer?

We should keep the present 28-day limit, and also keep the rule that prevents the police from questioning suspects after they have been charged	7%
The police should continue to be barred from questioning suspects after they have been charged, but the time limit for holding suspects without charge should be raised to 42 days	13%
The 28-day limit should remain, but the police should be allowed to question suspects further after they have been charged, if the police obtain fresh evidence on related offences	70%
Don't know	10%

% 0 · 10 · 20 · 30 · 40 · 50 · 60 · 70

Fieldwork: 25-27 March 2008. Sample size: 1926. Source: YouGov (www.yougov.com)

Public attitudes to human rights

Commission announces independent Inquiry into human rights and British attitudes to them

Trevor Phillips today announces the launch of an independent inquiry into human rights in Britain.

The inquiry will be chaired by Dame Nuala O'Loan, the former Northern Ireland Police Ombudsman who led the investigation into the Omagh bombings. Trevor Phillips said that the inquiry will be 'a full, frank and most importantly independent appraisal' of how human rights works in Britain.

81% agree 'there are some problems with human rights in Britain'

The announcement comes as Britain approaches the 10th anniversary of the passing of the Human Rights Act and the 60th anniversary of the UN's Universal Declaration of Human Rights.

Yet despite human rights featuring in British law for nearly a decade, a GfK NOP poll for the Commission showed that the term 'human rights' still prompts blank or mixed reactions from a large proportion of the British public.

According to the poll, 40% have either not heard the phrase 'human rights', are unable to name any of the protected rights or don't know if they support the legislation. Nevertheless, 47% supported 'human rights' laws in Britain.

The poll showed:
⇨ 56% agree that 'people only talk about their human rights when they're trying to get something they're not entitled to'.
⇨ 68% agree that the government is 'more concerned about the human rights of minority groups than those of the average person'.
⇨ 81% agree 'there are some problems with human rights in Britain'.
⇨ Only 23% agree that 'the media reports human rights stories fairly'.
⇨ Among those who were familiar with the term 'human rights' and who understood what at least one of their rights would be, the majority were supportive.*

The Commission's inquiry will separate myth from reality, confronting and engaging both critics and supporters. In addition to traditional in-depth research, public polling and focus group work, the Commission will convene a series of public evidence sessions where it will hear from expert witnesses.

The inquiry will look at what drives public perceptions of human rights and whether the Human Rights Act leads to tangible benefits in the way that public services are provided.

The final report is expected in Spring 2009.

Trevor Phillips said:

'Since the Human Rights Act came into force it has faced many criticisms and some would say it has lacked a powerful advocate. Too many now view it as a charter for miscreants, especially criminals, terrorists and others trying to exploit the system.

'The Commission has an important role to play in separating myth from reality and embarking on a full, frank and most importantly independent assessment of human rights in Britain. Interestingly, there is some anecdotal evidence to suggest that once the individual aspects of human rights are explained the public feel more positive about the issue.

'But our role is not simply that of advocate, challenging the perception that human rights doesn't bring

benefits to a wide range of people. We will also act as critical friend, exposing any barriers that – in reality – mean human rights are not enjoyed by as wide a range of people as they should be, for example those in private care homes.'

Dame Nuala O'Loan said:

'I am delighted to be chairing this inquiry which is enormously important. It's about how these issues affect people like you and me at critical moments in our lives. Human rights must mean something to people. Clearly, we have an enormous challenge ahead. The polling conducted by the Commission indicates that there are some misunderstandings.

'The inquiry will be open and evidence based. The Commission has already laid some important groundwork, and I look forward to hearing from people in the evidence sessions, some of whom may have critical and challenging opinions. I expect there may even be some things that surprise us.'

60% of respondents understood the term 'human rights' and were then asked whether they were supportive of it. Of the sample, 79% were supportive of human rights. 17 October 2008

⇨ The above information is reprinted with kind permission from the Commission for Equality and Human Rights. Visit www.equalityhumanrights.com for more information.

© Commission for Equality and Human Rights

Facts about modern slavery

Information from Reuters

Two centuries after Britain's first act abolishing the slave trade received royal assent, trafficking in human flesh is still thriving, anti-slavery campaigners say.

Here are details of persistent slavery in the 21st century:

Some numbers

⇨ Slavery is officially banned internationally by all countries, yet despite this there are more slaves than ever before. Today there are an estimated 27 million slaves worldwide: people paid no money, locked away and controlled by violence.

⇨ An estimated 218 million children are used for labour, United Nations Children's Fund UNICEF says. Millions work in especially horrific circumstances, including the virtual slavery of bonded labour.

⇨ An estimated 126 million children work in the worst forms of child labour – one in 12 of the world's 5- to 17-year-olds.

⇨ There are around 300,000 child soldiers involved in over 30 areas of conflict worldwide, some younger than 10 years old.

Types of slavery

⇨ Bonded labour – People become bonded labourers by taking or being tricked into taking a loan for as little as the cost of medicine for a sick child. To repay the debt, many are forced to work long hours, and sometimes all year. They receive basic food and shelter as 'payment' for their work, but many may never pay off the loan, which can be passed down for generations.

⇨ Forced labour – People are illegally recruited by individuals, governments or political parties and forced to work, usually under threat of violence or other penalties.

⇨ Trafficking – The transport and/ or trade of women, children and men from one area to another for the purpose of forcing them into

conditions of slavery. Human trafficking ranks as the second largest criminal industry globally, second only to drug smuggling, and equal with illegal weapons transactions.

Slavery now

⇨ The vast majority of the world's slaves are in South Asia, including India, Pakistan, Bangladesh and Nepal.

⇨ Millions of children in India are given up by their families into virtual slavery as domestic workers. Children are exploited by employers and made to do strenuous labour for little or no pay.

⇨ Despite a ban on employing children under 14, India's labour ministry recently said there are 12.6 million children aged between 5 and 14 working, the largest number of child labourers in the world.

Europe

⇨ British government research shows that during 2003 there were an estimated 4,000 victims of trafficking for prostitution in Britain. The figure has risen at least threefold since 1998, according to Home Office figures.

⇨ Romania and its southern neighbour Bulgaria are among 11 countries listed by the United Nations as top sources of human trafficking, based on reported numbers of victims. Sofia's interior ministry's organised crime unit said at the end of 2006 that 4,000-5,000 Bulgarian women are trafficked a year.

⇨ Other countries in the region, the poorest in Europe, are also hotbeds for organised crime and illegal trade such as Moldova and Ukraine.

Africa

⇨ Last July, ministers from 26 West and Central African countries launched a new attempt to

revitalise the fight against people trafficking, which fuels child labour and sexual exploitation in the region and beyond.

⇨ An estimated 200,000-800,000 people are trafficked each year in the sub-region. Children are moved within and between countries to work as domestics, in agriculture or in the markets. Women are tricked with promises of good jobs abroad into forced prostitution in Europe or the Middle East.

⇨ In Mauritania slavery was nominally abolished at independence in 1960 and legally banned again in 1981. Yet rights groups say it persists in the interior of the nation of 3 million inhabitants, many of them nomads.

⇨ Anti-Slavery International has estimated at least 43,000 people live as slaves across Niger, many of them born into slavery and working as domestic servants or farm labourers. Slaves receive only a meagre amount of food and are often victims of violence and sexual abuse.

Sources: Reuters/Anti-Slavery International/UNICEF/http:// freetheslaves.net
20 March 2007

Slavery in modern Britain

Comprehensive new JRF report shows that slavery exists in the UK today

As the UK marks the 200th anniversary of legislation for the abolition of the slave trade, a new report shows how modern forms of slavery occur in the UK. Written by leading experts in the field, this report is the first comprehensive review of evidence about the extent of slavery in the UK today.

Contemporary slavery in the UK, produced by a joint research team from the University of Hull and Anti-Slavery International for the Joseph Rowntree Foundation (JRF), examines the nature of modern slavery and the conditions under which it occurs. It also contains detailed accounts of the circumstances being faced by those enslaved.

The report shows that contemporary slavery in the UK exists in various forms, particularly as a result of trafficking. All forms share elements of the exploitative relationship which have historically constituted slavery: severe economic exploitation; the lack of a human rights framework; and one person's control over another through the prospect or reality of violence. Slavery is defined and prohibited under international law. Coercion distinguishes slavery from poor working conditions.

Archbishop Desmond Tutu, who has worked with the authors to raise awareness of modern slavery, said: 'I didn't know about all these forms that existed...It is hidden. Generally people would not believe that it is possible under modern conditions.'

UK enforcement agencies estimate there may be as many as 10,000 gangmasters operating across the various industrial sectors. Many operate legally but some do not. Many people trafficked into Britain and forced into slavery enter the country legally from countries in Europe, Africa, Asia and South America. They are then trafficked by agents into forced labour in such areas as agriculture, construction, cleaning and domestic work, food processing and packaging, care/nursing, hospitality and the restaurant trade, as well as into sexual exploitation.

Some UK-based companies, knowingly or not, rely on people working in slavery to produce goods that they sell: complex sub-contracting and supply chains, managed by agents elsewhere, often obscure this involvement.

The report claims that the UK has tended to address trafficking as an issue of migration control rather than one of human rights. Trafficked people are often subjected to forced labour through a mix of enforced debt, intimidation, the removal of documents and an inadequate understanding of their rights. Statutory agency personnel are often unsure how to assist trafficked migrant workers and keep few or no records as to their subsequent well-being.

'Current protection and support services for trafficked men, women and children are inadequate and there is no specific assistance available to those who are trafficked for labour exploitation. A review of the position of most organisations active in this field suggests that formal adoption by the UK Government of the various treaties and conventions in place would be an important first step,' said Professor Gary Craig, report co-author and Associate Director of the Wilberforce Institute for the study of Slavery and Emancipation (WISE) at the University of Hull.

'Migrant workers are particularly vulnerable to slavery and exploitation. The promotion of regular migration is essential to tackling this problem in the UK, as is ensuring the protection of migrant workers' rights. Our research indicates that the needs of victims seem to have been secondary to government policy; one interviewee commented that although the police see trafficked people as victims, the immigration service sees them as illegal entrants,' added Aidan McQuade, report co-author and Director of Anti-Slavery International.

Slavery in contemporary Britain cannot be seen in isolation. Most of those working as slaves in the UK have come from elsewhere, often legally. This makes slavery an international issue. Many relationships of enslavement trap people by withdrawing their passports or ID documents, making escape unlikely. Evidence shows that those who protest about the appalling working conditions may be beaten, abused, raped, deported or even killed.

Contemporary slavery in the UK exists in various forms, particularly as a result of trafficking

---

The report recommends national action complemented by international law and collaborative cooperation, with policy and service responses that regard those in slavery as victims first and foremost, rather than as criminals. It argues for a more robust stance against the exploiters and for proper resources for enforcement agencies. It concludes that training in awareness of how to identify slavery conditions for local service providers and a public awareness campaign are also needed.

Notes

1 The report's publication coincides with an exhibition on the past and present slave trade and a service at York Minster led by Archbishop John Sentamu.

2 The full report, *Contemporary slavery in the UK: Overview and key issues*, by the Joseph Rowntree Foundation is available to download or buy.

26 February 2007

⇨ The above press release is reprinted with kind permission from the Joseph Rowntree Foundation. Visit www.jrf.org.uk for more information.

© Joseph Rowntree Foundation

Trafficking cases

Information from Amnesty International

All of the cases below are recognised by the United Nations as contemporary forms of slavery and in most of these and other such cases UK nationals are complicit in the abuses suffered. All the victims in these cases need time and support to recover from what they have been through and the European Convention can help put victims first, help prosecute the abusers and help deter the trade.

No more excuses: the UK must sign the Convention.

Case 1 – sexual exploitation

'Maryam' was ostracised by her family when she refused to undergo female genital mutilation prior to a likely forced marriage after her twin sister had died of the same procedure in Africa. She was picked up by a child trafficker at age 13 and brought to London where she was locked in a basement and suffered repeated rape as a child prostitute. At 19, possibly being now too 'old' for her trafficker's clients, he provided her with false documents and let her go. She tried to leave the country on those documents and was arrested and convicted. She served a 10-month prison sentence. Although she was keen to see her trafficker brought to justice, police response has been very slow and inadequate to date.

Case 2 – forced labour

In February 2004, a group of Greek workers were brought to Cornwall to pick daffodils for major retailers including Marks and Spencer. They had to work 10 hours a day in snow and rain, they were given cans of dog food to eat and accommodated in tents and unheated sheds. They alleged that they had been beaten and threatened at gunpoint before they managed to escape (*Independent* newspaper).

Case 3 – debt bondage

Jin Lai, 16, was found on the street and taken to the police station. He had been living and working in a restaurant 7 days a week before he managed to run away. Jin was living in debt-bondage forced to work for free until he had 'paid off' those who had arranged his family's passage to the UK (UNICEF 2005).

Case 4 – domestic work and sexual abuse

Adina's parents died when she was 15 and she went to work on her Aunt's market stall. One day her Aunt told her to go with 2 men who would bring her to the UK for 'a better life'. Here, she was taken to a house where she was locked up and forced to perform all domestic labour. She was also raped. She was kept locked in the kitchen with access to a toilet and basin only and did not know where she was. She was 17 by the time she managed to escape (UNICEF 2005). *Updated 24 April 2007*

⇨ The above information is reprinted with kind permission from Amnesty International. Visit www.amnesty.org. uk for more information.

© Amnesty International

Human rights in a time of terror

At the beginning of a year that brings together the Beijing Olympics and the 60th anniversary of the Universal Declaration of Human Rights, David Ransom assesses the damage done by the 'War on Terror' to the one race that really counts

If the torture of a single person could save the lives of a thousand others, would it be justified? Difficult to say 'no'. But that must be said all the same, because torture has never saved anyone from anything; not from a single suicide bomb, not from a single act of terrorism or fate worse than torture itself. So why should anyone be asked to suppose that it might? Who can believe that it does?

Morality and belief may matter, but without knowledge and reason they readily produce a grief-stricken mess. The so-called War on Terror is a prime example. Britain really did invade Iraq in pursuit of weapons of mass destruction that did not exist, at the bidding of little more than the moral convictions of a semi-detached Prime Minister. In the absence of any supporting evidence whatsoever, the British Government still persists in trying to extend detention without trial, purportedly in response to the

> **If the torture of a single person could save the lives of a thousand others, would it be justified?**

wishes of the police. On the basis of unspecified official beliefs about what they might do next, people in Britain can now find themselves under house arrest that may never end, on charges they never hear and evidence they cannot challenge in a court they cannot attend.

Not the United States

When a US President takes it upon himself to convict terrorists or invent 'enemy combatants' then the result is quite likely to be even messier. In Not the United States (Guantánamo Bay), three-quarters of the people kidnapped from Afghanistan and Pakistan were not even plausible terrorists, but taxi drivers and the like detained more or less at random, frequently by local bounty hunters responding to 80 million air-dropped leaflets promising hefty rewards.[1] An unknown number of people have been 'disappeared' to enable the extraction of useless information by torture – a passable re-enactment, this, of life under the jackboots of Latin America, which gave rise to a quite specific international prohibition on the practice.

In the US 'Homeland' the Constitution and the Bill of Rights are mere irritants to ideologues for whom 9/11 was not a catastrophe but a godsend. The Patriot Act, passed in just six weeks after 9/11, massively extended the Executive's powers without any serious examination of precisely how such powers would have averted the original disaster.[2] Swelling and unaccountable private armies, like Blackwater, don't just shoot up civilians in Iraq, but were among the first to appear, fully armed, on the streets of New Orleans after Hurricane Katrina.[3]

Trumped up

All this suggests that the War on Terror is not just morally adrift but entirely misconceived. After all, it is founded on the notion that 'national security' must somehow trump human rights. Even supposing that rights were a tradable commodity, which they are not, the deal can never be completed, because human rights and human security are not mutually exclusive but mutually

dependent. The less the general respect for human rights, the greater the general experience of insecurity – and the more the War on Terror escalates its own self-perpetuating spiral. Shameful as 9/11 and suicide bombings truly are, nothing is less likely to counteract them than a disproportionate response in the same suit. At least since the Universal Declaration of Human Rights in 1948, and hard as many have tried, no one has succeeded in demonstrating otherwise.

Slow and frustrating though it may have been, steady and significant progress really was being made on human rights. The protection of international law was gradually extended to women, ethnic groups, children, disabled people, migrant workers and indigenous peoples. Following the Vienna conference in 1993, international 'machinery' – courts and tribunals – finally began to track down petty tyrants and psychopaths, who would no longer be quite so free to cultivate the fruits of their numbered foreign bank accounts.

Lowest point

Yet this year, the Declaration's 60th anniversary, comes at perhaps the lowest point in its history, characterised as it is more aptly by the repellent execution of Saddam Hussein than by the overthrow of a malign dictator. We have entered an 'American Century' of war without end, waged primarily by the very same states that were instrumental in making the Declaration in 1948 specifically to avoid war altogether.

It's not as if there is any lack of work still to be undertaken. With the Cold War done and dusted, the 'positive' or 'collective' rights set out in the Declaration's social and economic clauses remain spectacularly unrealised. Millions of children still experience the madness of hunger and death before they can have the faintest notion of their rights as a child. The right to life is not to be found in the absence of clean water to drink. The Declaration itself is of little use to those who can't read it.

Lest we forget, Article 26 states categorically: 'Education shall be free, at least in the elementary and fundamental stages.' So what can the over-educated suits of the World Bank and IMF have been thinking of when, throughout the 1980s and 1990s, they routinely imposed fees for elementary education on the poorest people in the world? Not an indictment for the abuse of human rights, you can be sure.

Beijing blues

The reversal is made more telling by the coincidence of the Declaration's anniversary with the Beijing Olympics. When the International Olympic Committee chose Beijing for 2008 it struck a deal that included a commitment from the Chinese Government to 'improve' on human rights. But, since the details have been kept secret, the deal is meaningless.

Meanwhile, China maintains its material support for murderous regimes in Sudan and Burma, a repressive occupation of Tibet, a predilection for indiscriminate

We need to limit democratic freedoms to safeguard democracy.

NO WAR

executions and the suppression of internal dissent. Some reluctance to participate in the Games - if not a boycott - might reasonably have been anticipated, but very little response of any kind has come from governments. So it has been left to others, including some of those who are campaigning for the people of Tibet, Burma or Darfur, to make their own.[4]

It is quite reasonable to argue - as many Chinese and international human rights groups have done, thus far - that the Games offer some kind of opening to the 'international community' which will benefit the Chinese people. But an elusive international community, transfixed by the War on Terror, is no longer preoccupied with human rights. Rather, China has become so central to

the process of corporate globalisation that all other considerations have been dropped like a stone. The deep-seated addiction of corporate globalisation to the abuse of human rights does little to suggest that the Games themselves - heavily reliant as they are on corporate sponsorship - will do much for the Chinese people at all.

Race for rights

Even if the Olympics won't come to human rights, human rights can still stage their own Olympics. The races that count will not take place in Beijing in August, duly fuelled by the likes of Coca-Cola and environmental destruction, but continuously on the streets, in the fields and the homes of millions of people who know what it means to be human.

Notes

1 Andy Worthington, *The Guantánamo Files*, Pluto Press, London, 2007.
2 Barbara Olshansky, *Democracy Detained*, Seven Stories Press, New York, 2007.
3 Jeremy Scahill, *Blackwater – the rise of the world's most powerful mercenary army*, Serpent's Tail, London, 2007.
4 For a brief account of the hesitant boycott movement, see http://en.wikipedia.org/wiki/2008SummerOlympics

January 2008

⇨ Reprinted by kind permission of New Internationalist. Copyright *New Internationalist*. www.newint.org

© New Internationalist

Public support for terror measures

Migration Watch – big majority for human rights opt-out over terror threat

There is overwhelming public support for a much tougher line to be taken against terrorists and suspected terrorists including withdrawal from the European Convention on Human Rights, reveals a new poll out today.

A YouGov poll conducted on behalf of think-tank Migration Watch showed that, when asked if the UK should renounce its membership of the Convention in order to have greater powers to deal with suspected and convicted terrorists, 61% agreed. Just 26% supported the proposition that Britain should remain a member of the Human Rights Convention, and not reduce human rights in response to the terrorist threat.

There was even greater support for the proposal that, having withdrawn, we should issue a warning and then deport convicted terrorists without further appeal - even to countries where they might face torture, with 67% in favour and 18% against. This view was held fairly uniformly across the UK and within different social groups, although the opposition to

it among younger people was in the mid-20s.

When asked if Britain should have, and use, the right to deport foreigners suspected by the intelligence services, even if there is not enough courtroom evidence to bring them to trial, and they might be sent to countries where they could be tortured, 55% said we should while 26% were opposed.

There was a stronger response when asked whether Britain should have, and use, the right to imprison foreign terrorist suspects for as long as the authorities judge necessary, unless they choose to return to their home countries, with a massive 75% supporting the proposition and just 13% opposed.

'These results demonstrate that the British people are tired of seeing the interests of those intent on destroying our way of life being put before the safety of themselves and their families,' said Sir Andrew Green, chairman of Migration Watch.

'Most people find it totally incomprehensible that convicted terrorists are able to remain in Britain

after they have completed their prison sentences. Our continued membership also means we have lost the ability to remove people from this country even when there is good intelligence that their presence here is a real or potential risk to public safety.

There is overwhelming public support for a much tougher line to be taken against terrorists

---

'We accept that the ECHR was right for the time in which it was created, 50 years ago, but we are now in an entirely new situation and the public clearly believe that it is time that this new reality was recognised - and acted upon,' he said.

23 July 2007

⇨ Reprinted with kind permission from Migration Watch. Visit www.migrationwatch.org.uk for more.

© Migration Watch

Torture: myths and facts

Information from the Medical Foundation for the Care of Victims of Torture

Myths about torture

Universally deplored, torture was once a practice that provoked unwavering condemnation. States that used torture to repress their citizens were reviled and called to account by the international community. Yet in recent years some have sought to justify the use of torture as a means to the end of keeping the public safe from harm. Much of the debate has been prompted by the global threat of terrorism, which is undoubtedly a serious and pressing issue. By pitching national security against the use of torture some governments and leading thinkers have sought to dress up torture as 'interrogation' or to legitimise its use.

The current misleading and inaccurate information surrounding the issue of torture has given rise to a new mythology. Here we seek to dispel some of those myths and describe the reality of torture that we see through the experience of our clients from countries around the world.

MYTH: *Torture works*

FACT: It has been accepted since the time of Plato that torture is categorically ineffective in extracting information.

In the experience of thousands of survivors seen by the MF, most people subjected to extreme levels of psychological and physical pain and suffering will say anything and even sign false confessions to make the torture stop. Any information which may be extracted under torture is therefore unreliable. This scenario was actively played out in the case of the 'Tipton three', who while held in Guantánamo Bay confessed to meeting Osama bin Laden, despite being in the UK at the relevant time. They were ultimately released without charge.

Information extracted under torture is also inadmissible in a court of law. Under Article 15 of the UN Convention against Torture and Other Cruel, Inhuman or Degrading Treatment or Punishment, 'any statement which is established to have been made as a result of torture shall not be invoked as evidence in any proceedings, except against a person accused of torture as evidence that the statement was made'.

> **In recent years some have sought to justify the use of torture as a means to the end of keeping the public safe from harm**

MYTH: *Torture is a means to an end*

FACT: The 'ticking time bomb' argument is that if by torturing a person a catastrophe could be avoided, then torturing that person would be an acceptable means of saving the lives of thousands of others. The human rights of one person are pitched against the safety of thousands in an emotionally persuasive argument that has garnered much support in the wake of 9/11 and the climate of fear of war and terrorism.

However, the scenario is a hypothetical extreme with no basis in reality. It also presupposes that torture would be limited to one particular incident and that, in fact, the information sought to be gained would actually be proffered under torture. Yet as history shows, to permit any abhorrent practice once is to set a dangerous precedent. Most recently, this was seen when the 'enhanced interrogation techniques' used in Abu Ghraib were replicated in Guantánamo.

Torture not only degrades the victim, it degrades the torturer and the society that permits it. When governments condone torture they risk losing their legitimacy.

MYTH: *Only criminals and terrorists are tortured*

FACT: In 2007, the MF received requests for help from some 2,000 people who had fled 95 countries across the world.

The vast majority of MF clients report having been targeted due to their race, ethnic origin, gender, religious, cultural or political beliefs. Political activists and journalists are often targeted by the authorities for vocalising their opposition to government policies. Many others find themselves falsely implicated in terrorist incidents with which they had no involvement. Many people are targeted for torture during conflicts, where torture is used to instil a climate of fear and to force people to flee.

The husbands, wives and children of people targeted by state agents are frequently targeted simply by association in an effort to get to someone else. This has been particularly true for women fleeing torture in Sri Lanka. Significant numbers of the wives of men who were either members or suspected members of the Liberation Tamil Tigers of Tamil Elam (LTTE) reported to the MF how they were detained and tortured.

MYTH: *Rape is not torture*

FACT: Rape is classified as an act of torture within international human rights, humanitarian and criminal law, and is also recognised as a war crime or act of genocide.

The inclusion of rape in international legal standards acknowledges the severity of the act of rape as a method of torture, and recognises the need for greater protection for victims, particularly at times when they are most susceptible to infringement.

MYTH: *Only women are victims of rape*

FACT: Although women and girls are the predominant victims of rape, men and boys are also subjected to sexual abuse and rape. However, due to overwhelming feelings of shame, humiliation and cultural taboos, male rape often remains undisclosed.

For female victims, gang rape is a common experience reported. Many of the male clients seen by the MF describe being raped individually, by other men, while alone. In such cases, the torture has usually taken place when one man is in control of another, commonly in detention. Survivors have also reported being raped at home, or being abducted and raped in an isolated place.

MYTH: *The effects of torture are only temporary*

FACT: Torture often has lifelong physical and psychological consequences. Surviving torture is only the beginning of a long journey towards rehabilitation.

Torture can result in lasting physical injury, including permanent disability and scarring – inescapable reminders of the suffering endured by victims, which can exacerbate suffering and prolong the rehabilitation and treatment process.

Some survivors of sexual torture contract sexually transmitted diseases including HIV-AIDS, and some women become pregnant from rape, causing further trauma and life-changing consequences.

Many survivors seen by the MF receive care and treatment for post-traumatic stress disorder, anxiety, flashbacks, nightmares and insomnia. Depression, exacerbated by overwhelming senses of humiliation and shame, triggers suicidal tendencies in some survivors.

Having fled for survival, clients can feel extreme guilt for leaving family, friends and other victims behind. Other survivors find it difficult to form and maintain relationships, have physical contact and to trust other people.

MYTH: *Torture only has lasting effects for the victim*

FACT: The torturer's goal is to repress and dehumanise the victim. While the act of torture is directed at an individual, the effects are widespread, resonating with those

who are witnesses, others who may hear the torture taking place and the families and communities of torture survivors. Torture has a metastasising effect on the lives of any of those whom it touches – including the perpetrators.

The effects of torture can last a lifetime. In addition to post-traumatic stress disorder, depression, anxiety, flashbacks, nightmares and insomnia, torture survivors can end up avoiding interacting with other people and distancing themselves from the outside world.

Children of torture survivors may be forced to interpret the stories of their parents to the authorities, causing them to digest and repeat information which can have a traumatising effect. The family context of a torture survivor is profoundly changed, presenting often overwhelming challenges to those who have a family member who has survived torture.

More broadly, the consequences for societies where torture is condoned are severe. Where torture is tolerated as a seemingly useful and acceptable technique to keep communities safe or to repress others sets a dangerous precedent that human rights are an expendable commodity.

MYTH: *Detainees on hunger strike are force-fed for their own benefit*

FACT: In 2006, four United Nations special rapporteurs, reporting to the UN Commission of Human Rights, declared force-feeding amounted to torture under Article 1 of the UN Convention against Torture.

In its 1975 Declaration of Tokyo, the World Medical Assembly prohibited force-feeding advising 'where a prisoner refuses nourishment and is considered by the physician as capable of forming an unimpaired and rational judgment concerning the consequences of such a voluntary refusal of nourishment, he or she shall not be fed artificially'.

The WMA's subsequent 1991 Declaration of Malta reinforces that 'forced feeding contrary to an informed and voluntary refusal is unjustifiable' and recognises hunger strike as a 'form of protest by people who lack other

ways of making their demands known'.

Force-feeding involves forcibly restraining a person in order to insert a tube through the mouth or nose down to the stomach, causing extreme pain and often bleeding and vomiting.

In 2007, the MF joined calls for the American Medical Association to launch disciplinary hearings against any of its members that were found to be involved in the force-feeding of detainees held in Guantánamo.

MYTH: *Torture survivors are not detained in the UK*

FACT: The UK Government's Operation Enforcement Manual states that torture survivors should not be detained unless there are exceptional circumstances, and even then, detention should be an absolute last resort.

While data on the number of torture survivors who are detained is not readily available, in 2007 more than 150 asylum seekers were released from detention after being assessed by the MF following claims of torture in their country of origin. According to a report in March 2008 by the Immigration Asylum Commission (IAC), and as exemplified by cases referred to the MF, many torture survivors continue to be detained.

Being detained is not conducive to effective therapeutic work or rehabilitation. According to Dr Christina Pourgourides, a former MF psychiatrist, who investigated the effect of detention on mental health, 'for torture survivors the experience of detention may provoke feelings of fear and powerlessness and restimulate their distress'.

MYTH: 'Dawn raids' do not happen

FACT: 'Dawn raids' – the forcible removal of refused asylum-seeking families in the early hours of the morning without prior notification – is a method currently employed by the UK Border Agency and administered by its officials.

Families are either taken directly to the airport where they will be removed to their home country or to an Immigration Removal Centre where they await removal.

MF clients have reported being subjected to dawn raids. The MF has called for an immediate moratorium on dawn raids, which have been known to involve the handcuffing of children.

MYTH: 'Waterboarding' is a legal method of interrogation

FACT: Waterboarding is a terrifying and dangerous torture method that makes victims feels as though they are drowning. Held down with a cloth stuffed into their mouth, victims are forced to ingest water hosed or poured liberally over their nose and mouth. Victims take water into their lungs and suffer deprivation of oxygen to the brain and can very easily drown during this torture.

In February 2008 the US administration admitted to waterboarding three Guantánamo Bay detainees in 2003 and has justified this decision by maintaining that US Presidential orders to employ the practice take precedence over international human rights and humanitarian law.

This justification neither validates waterboarding as an acceptable interrogation method nor gives any legal basis for its use.

MYTH: Agents of the UK do not engage in torture

The murder of Baha Mousa and torture of nine others

FACT: In March 2008, the Ministry of Defence (MoD) admitted breaching the European Convention on Human Rights in relation to the death of an Iraqi civilian and the torture of nine others in September 2003.

In July 2008, the MoD paid the families almost £3 million in compensation for the murder of Baha Mousa and the torture and abuse of nine others.

The family of Iraqi receptionist Mr Mousa brought the action against the MoD following his death and a coroner's report which identified 93 separate injuries to his body.

Over three years and at a cost of £20 million, the MoD argued that troops on overseas operations were not covered by European human rights law – an argument ultimately dismissed by the UK House of Lords.

A court martial hearing found that troops had ignored the 1972 ruling by the UK government which banned the use of hooding, stress positions and deprivation of food, noise and sleep. One soldier pleaded guilty to inhumane treatment and six others, including the commanding officer, were acquitted of negligence and abuse. No one was convicted of killing Mr Mousa.

In May 2008 the MoD agreed to an independent public inquiry into the deaths, to investigate whether there is a systemic failure within the army and its training systems.

Alleged outsourcing of torture by UK to Pakistan

FACT: In July 2008, MPs called for an investigation into allegations that Britain had 'outsourced' torture of its citizens to Pakistani authorities. Three British men allege they were arrested and tortured in Pakistan over lengths varying from 16 days to five months before eventually being released without charge.

MPs called for the Intelligence and Security Committee, which oversees MI5 and MI6, to investigate the allegations.

MYTH: Evidence obtained under torture can be used in a court of law

FACT: The MF played a pivotal role in successfully advocating for evidence obtained under torture to be deemed inadmissible in British judicial proceedings, deemed illegal in December 2005.

A unanimous ruling by the House of Lords in 2005 overturned an earlier judgment by the Court of Appeal and the Special Immigration Appeals Commission which ruled that the state had no obligation to investigate how evidence is produced. The Lords rejected those judgments saying that if a court thinks 'on a balance of probabilities' that evidence before it has been obtained through torture, it must rule it out.

Under Article 15 of the UN Convention against Torture and Other Cruel, Inhuman or Degrading Treatment or Punishment, 'any statement which is established to have been made as a result of torture shall not be invoked as evidence in any proceedings, except against a person accused of torture as evidence that the statement was made'.

The use of evidence obtained under torture is also in breach of Article 6 of the European Convention on Human Rights, which guarantees a person a fair trial.

MYTH: The UK has had no involvement in extraordinary rendition

FACT: In February 2008 the UK government admitted that it had received confirmation from Washington that US aircraft had landed at Diego Garcia, the British Indian Ocean Territory where the US has a large military base. Destined for Guantánamo Bay and Morocco, both aircraft carried a sole detainee and landed at Diego Garcia in 2002.

⇨ The above information is reprinted with kind permission from the Medical Foundation for the Care of Victims of Torture. Visit www.torturecare.org.uk for more information.

© *Medical Foundation for the Care of Victims of Torture*

Children's rights

Information from UNICEF

Why do children's rights need protection?

Every child and young person under 18 has rights and responsibilities. They're protected by the United Nations Convention on the Rights of the Child. It's been signed by every country in the world, except the USA and Somalia.

The Convention begins by talking about the reasons why it's needed:

⇨ Because children are individuals and members of their families and communities. They have rights and responsibilities, appropriate to their age and development.

⇨ Because recognising everyone's rights is vital for a world full of freedom, justice and peace.

⇨ Because children need special care and protection.

⇨ Because families play a really important role in society. Children develop best if their families give them love, understanding, and happiness.

⇨ Because children should grow up 'in the spirit of peace, dignity, tolerance, freedom, equality and solidarity'.

⇨ Because, in all countries of the world, there are children living in exceptionally difficult conditions. These children need special help.

⇨ Because children's cultures and traditions should be protected.

⇨ Because the world needs to work together to make life better for children, especially children in the world's poorest countries.

Your rights under the UNCRC

The Convention spells out your rights in a series of 'articles'.

Article 1
Everyone under the age of 18 has all the rights in this Convention.

Article 2
The Convention applies to everyone whatever their race, religion, abilities, whatever they think or say, no matter what type of family they come from.

Article 3
All organisations concerned with children should work towards what is best for you.

Article 4
Governments should make these rights available to you.

Article 5
Governments should respect the rights and responsibilities of families to direct and guide their children so that, as they grow, they learn to use their rights properly.

Article 6
You have the right to life. Governments should ensure that children survive and develop healthily.

Article 7
You have the right to a legally registered name and nationality. You also have the right to know and, as far as possible, to be cared for by your parents.

Article 8
Governments should respect children's right to a name, a nationality and family ties.

Article 9
You should not be separated from your parents unless it is for your own good – for example, if a parent is mistreating or neglecting you. If your parents have separated, you have the right to stay in contact with both parents, unless this might harm you.

Article 10
Families who live in different countries should be allowed to move between those countries so that parents and children can stay in contact or get back together as a family.

Article 11
Governments should take steps to stop children being taken out of their own country illegally.

Article 12
You have the right to say what you think should happen when adults are making decisions that affect you, and to have your opinions taken into account.

Article 13
You have the right to get, and to share, information as long as the information is not damaging to yourself or others.

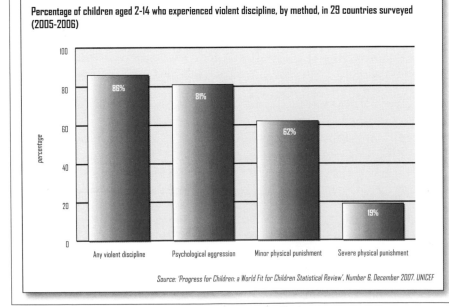

Violent discipline of children

Percentage of children aged 2-14 who experienced violent discipline, by method, in 29 countries surveyed (2005-2006)

Any violent discipline 86%
Psychological aggression 81%
Minor physical punishment 62%
Severe physical punishment 19%

Source: 'Progress for Children: a World Fit for Children Statistical Review', Number 6, December 2007, UNICEF

Article 14
You have the right to think and believe what you want and to practise your religion, as long as you are not stopping other people from enjoying their rights. Parents should guide children on these matters.

Article 15
You have the right to meet with other children and young people and to join groups and organisations, as long as this does not stop other people from enjoying their rights.

Article 16
You have the right to privacy. The law should protect you from attacks against your way of life, your good name, your family and your home.

Recognising everyone's rights is vital for a world full of freedom, justice and peace

---

Article 17
You have the right to reliable information from the mass media. Television, radio, and newspapers should provide information that you can understand, and should not promote materials that could harm you.

Article 18
Both parents share responsibility for bringing up their children, and should always consider what is best for each child. Governments should help parents by providing services to support them, especially if both parents work.

Article 19
Governments should ensure that children are properly cared for, and protect them from violence, abuse and neglect by their parents or anyone else who looks after them.

Article 20
If you cannot be looked after by your own family, you must be looked after properly, by people who respect your religion, culture and language.

Article 21
If you are adopted, the first concern must be what is best for you. The same rules should apply whether the adoption takes place in the country where you were born or if you move to another country.

Article 22
If you are a child who has come into a country as a refugee, you should have the same rights as children born in that country.

Article 23
If you have a disability, you should receive special care and support so that you can live a full and independent life.

Article 24
You have the right to good quality health care and to clean water, nutritious food and a clean environment so that you can stay healthy. Rich countries should help poorer countries achieve this.

Article 25
If you are looked after by your local authority rather than your parents, you should have your situation reviewed regularly.

Article 26
The government should provide extra money for the children of families in need.

Article 27
You have a right to a standard of living that is good enough to meet your physical and mental needs. The government should help families who cannot afford to provide this.

Article 28
You have a right to an education. Discipline in schools should respect children's human dignity. Primary education should be free. Wealthy countries should help poorer countries achieve this.

Article 29
Education should develop your personality and talents to the full. It should encourage you to respect your parents, your own and other cultures.

Article 30
You have a right to learn and use the language and customs of your family whether or not these are shared by the majority of the people in the country where you live.

Article 31
You have a right to relax, play and join in a wide range of activities.

Article 32
The government should protect you from work that is dangerous or might harm your health or education.

Article 33
The government should provide ways of protecting you from dangerous drugs.

Article 34
The government should protect you from sexual abuse.

Article 35
The government should ensure that you are not abducted or sold.

Article 36
You should be protected from any activities that could harm your development.

Article 37
If you break the law, you should not be treated cruelly. You should not be put in a prison with adults and you should be able to keep in contact with your family.

Article 38
Governments should not allow children under 16 to join the army. In war zones, you should receive special protection.

Article 39
If you have been neglected or abused, you should receive special help to restore your self-respect.

Article 40
If you are accused of breaking the law, you should receive legal help. Prison sentences for children should only be used for the most serious offences.

Article 41
If the laws of a particular country protect you better than the articles of the Convention, then those laws should stay.

Article 42
The government should make the Convention known to all parents and children.

Articles 43-54
are about how adults and governments should work together to make sure all children get all their rights.

Your call
All people have rights, but also the responsibility to make sure their behaviour doesn't stop others getting their rights.

⇨ The above information is reprinted with kind permission from UNICEF. Visit www.unicef.org.uk for more information.

Children's rights – the facts

Interesting facts and figures

If, like us, you love to collect facts and figures about children's rights, here's something to get you started:

⇨ Young people can vote from the age of 16 years in Brazil, Cuba, Nicaragua and the Isle of Man.

⇨ Eighteen countries have changed the law to stop parents hitting their children (the date in brackets is when the law was changed) – Sweden (1979), Finland (1983), Norway (1987), Austria (1989), Cyprus (1994), Denmark (1997), Latvia (1998), Croatia (1999), Germany (2000), Bulgaria (2000), Israel (2000), Iceland (2003), Romania (2004), Ukraine (2004), Hungary (2005), Greece (2006), the Netherlands (2007) and New Zealand (2007).

⇨ England has one of the lowest ages in Europe for when children can be charged by the police with committing a crime and taken to court – just 10 years. Young people cannot legally buy a pet or fireworks until they are 18 years.

⇨ There are over four billion children and young people in the world.

⇨ Babies born in the richest countries are expected to live until they are about 79 years; in the poorest countries life expectancy is just 53 years.

⇨ There are 3.9 million children and young people in the UK living in poverty.

⇨ The first country that agreed to follow the Convention on the Rights of the Child was Ghana in Africa (February 1990). The UK agreed to follow it in December 1991.

⇨ For every 100,000 children and young people in the UK, 23 are locked up. This is nearly four times the number of children and young people locked up in France and over 100 times the number of children locked up in Finland!

⇨ Over 8,600 children and young people were permanently excluded from school in 2006/07. Almost a thousand of these students attended primary school and 40 of them were aged just 5.

⇨ Norway was the first country to appoint an independent Children's Ombudsperson (in 1981) – a powerful person separate from government who can push for the rights of children and young people.

⇨ In 1669, children and young people petitioned Parliament to ask for an end to harsh and brutal treatment from teachers. Yet it wasn't until 1986 that a law was passed to stop teachers from using any kind of corporal punishment. The proposal was won in Parliament by just one vote!

⇨ Iran did have the lowest voting age, at 15, but it raised this to 18 in 2007.

⇨ Estonia in Northern Europe has the smallest child population in the world, at less than half a million. China and India have the biggest populations of children and young people, at close to 345 million each.

⇨ There are moves in Austria to lower the voting age to 16.

⇨ In England, the voting age was last reduced in 1967, from 21 to 18.

⇨ England has over 11 million children and young people – about one in five of the population!

⇨ The above information is reprinted with kind permission from the Children's Rights Alliance for England. Visit www.getreadyforchange.org.uk for more information.

© Children's Rights Alliance for England

Child labour

Information from UNICEF

Many children work. After school hours children can help with household chores, fetch water, run errands, or look after their younger brothers and sisters. In this way they can participate in family life and contribute to the family income. In doing so they pick up useful skills, learn more about their own communities and prepare themselves for the responsibilities of adult life. 'Child labour', however, implies something different – that children are doing things that are harmful to their healthy development. They may be labouring long hours, sacrificing time and energy that they might have spent at school or at home, enjoying the free and formative experience of childhood.

The impact on a child

Crucially, children working for long hours are missing out on the vital opportunity that education provides to equip themselves with the knowledge, life skills and confidence to participate fully in the economic and social development of their communities and to improve their own lives. In the worst cases, they may be doing work that is physically, emotionally and/or psychologically dangerous, putting their young bodies and minds under terrible strain that can lead to permanent damage.

Most people would agree that some types of child work are evidently wrong – working in coal mines, or rubbish tips, or glass factories. But other cases are less clear-cut. Much will depend on the age of the child: clearly there are some tasks that a child of sixteen might reasonably do that would be far more harmful for a child of six or eight.

The extent of the problem

How many child labourers are there? There will never be a definitive answer to this question, given inconsistencies in national standards and definitions as well as weaknesses in data collection. The most comprehensive global statistics on child labour come from the ILO (International Labour Organisation), which estimated that in 2002, the number of children worldwide who were 'economically active' – doing some type of work – amounted to 352 million. Of these, 211 million were aged 5-14. But whether this activity constitutes 'child labour' depends both on the nature of the work and the age of the child. Of the 352 million economically active children, the ILO counted 246 million as 'child labourers'.

Thus some 16% of the world's children are caught up in child labour and around one in twelve children are engaged either in hazardous work or in the very worst forms of child labour. Boys and girls appear to be working to a similar extent. Girls make up around half of all child labourers, though they make up a slightly smaller proportion – around 45% – of those engaged in hazardous work.

Where are the child workers and what do they do?

Child labourers are certainly not confined to poor countries. In the industrial countries, around 2.5 million children aged 5-14 are economically active, or around 2% of the total child population. In countries with transition economies, including former socialist countries, 2.4 million children aged 5-14, or around 4% of the total child population, are economically active. Nevertheless, the largest numbers of working children are to be found in the developing world. The most serious problems are in sub-Saharan Africa where 29% of children aged 5-14 are working (48 million), followed by Asia and the Pacific (19% or 127.3 million), Latin America and the Caribbean (16% or 17.4 million), and the Middle East and North Africa (15% or 13.4 million).

These children take on a huge variety of tasks. The majority work in agriculture, which employs 70% of child workers. This is followed by 8% working in manufacturing, and a further 8% in wholesale and retail trade, restaurants, hotels, and in various services. Most of the latter activities are performed in urban centres.

Why children work

Children work primarily because the environment they live in has failed to protect them from exploitation. A large number of factors interact to influence whether or not children will be working. These include:

⇨ Persistent poverty – in overall terms, the dominant issue is poverty. In countries with an annual per capita income of $500 or less, the proportion of children who are working is usually between 30% and 60%, while for countries with incomes between $500 and $1,000, the proportion drops to between 10% and 30%.

⇨ Economic shocks – a sudden family disaster, particularly death or illness, may force children to leave school and work. HIV/AIDS has now become a major factor, especially in Africa where over 28 million people are living with the disease. HIV/AIDS generally kills the main wage earners and shifts more of the income-earning burden to children.

⇨ Inadequate education – there is a close link between education and child labour. Education – particularly free and compulsory education of good quality up to the minimum age for entering into employment – is a key tool in preventing child labour. Attendance at school removes children, in part at least, from the labour market. As well as laying the basis for the acquisition of employable skills needed for gainful employment, school is also a place where children can be made aware of some of the risks inherent in their interaction with unscrupulous adults. The skills acquired at school may lead directly to the sort of gainful employment that will help children rise above the poverty into which

they were born – and thus make them, and their own children in turn, less exposed to exploitation. Furthermore, when children who have had the benefits of an education – particularly girls – grow up, they are more likely to make the choice of education for their own children, thus helping to reduce the future ranks of child labourers. Educated girls also marry later, have fewer unwanted pregnancies, and their children have lower infant mortality rates because of better health practices – all of which will contribute to breaking the cycle of poverty that underpins the ready supply of child labourers.

⇨ The demand for child labour – children may be pushed into work by poverty or the lack of alternatives but they can also be pulled towards work. Employers are often keen to recruit children since they will work more cheaply than adults and are likely to be more submissive. If the 'employers' are the parents, then the children's labour is free. In addition, employers may consider that some tasks are particularly suitable for children – running errands for example.

⇨ The above information is re-printed with kind permission from UNICEF. Visit www.unicef.org.uk for more information.

© UNICEF

Widespread forms of child slavery

Most widespread forms of child slavery revealed by new Save the Children report

On the 200th anniversary of the Slave Trade Act, a new report by Save the Children reveals millions of children are still living as child slaves.

The report exposes the eight most prevalent forms of child slavery that are still condemning children to live in appalling conditions, forced to work long hours for little or nothing in return and often subject to extreme harm, violence and rape.

Child trafficking

- 1.2 million children and babies are trafficked every year, including into Western Europe, the Americas and the Caribbean, and the number is increasing.
- Gangs involved in child and people trafficking make an estimated profit of US$ 32 billion per year.

Child prostitution

- At any one time across the world, around 1.8 million children are being abused through prostitution, child pornography and sex tourism.
- In the UK there are 5,000 child prostitutes. 75 per cent of them are girls.

Bonded child labour

- Millions of children are forced to work away their childhood in horrific conditions to pay off debt, or simply the interest on it.
- In India alone, estimates suggest up to 15 million children could be enslaved by somebody else's debt, many involved in illegal, hazardous and dangerous work.

Forced work in mines

- One million children are risking their lives in mines and quarries in more than 50 African, Asian and South American countries.
- In the Sahel region of Africa, 200,000 children are daily risking their lives in gold and mineral mines.

Agricultural labour

- 132 million children under 15 are trapped working in agriculture, often exposed to pesticides, heavy machinery, machetes and axes.
- In Kazakhstan, children work in cotton and tobacco fields and factories for up to 12 hours a day, seven days a week.

Child soldiers

- 300,000 children under 15 are involved with fighting forces, including government armies. Boys and girls in at least 13 countries are actively being recruited as child soldiers or as army 'wives'.
- Around 11,000 children in Democratic Republic of Congo are currently being held by fighting groups.

Forced child marriage

- Child marriage, which often includes mail order and internet brides, is one of the most widespread – yet hidden – forms of slavery. Girls as young as four are forced to live and have sex with their husband, and are often kept trapped indoors.
- Girls under 15 are five times more likely to die during pregnancy and childbirth than women over 20. In

In the UK there are 5,000 child prostitutes. 75 per cent of them are girls

Afghanistan more than half of all girls are married before they are 16.

Domestic slavery

- Millions of children across the world, some as young as six, are forced to work up to 15-hour days as domestic workers. Many are beaten, starved and sexually abused.
- There are 200,000 child domestic workers in Kenya, 550,000 in Brazil and 264,000 in Pakistan.

Jasmine Whitbread, CEO Save the Children:

'Child slavery is not a historical phenomenon – it is a stark reality for millions of children in both poor and rich countries. These children are treated like commodities; they can be lent or sold to other owners without warning, and live under crushing conditions of humiliation and abuse. Governments everywhere – including the UK – are not doing enough to respond to the plight of children in this inhumane situation. World leaders and international donors must act as a matter of urgency to address child slavery and put in place the laws and resources needed to eradicate these terrible practices.'

Save the Children is calling on all governments to:
⇨ address and ensure the eradication of child slavery through their own policies on global poverty reduction.
⇨ invest sufficient money and resources to protect children associated with slavery.
⇨ implement international standards on the worst forms of child labour where children in slavery are found.
⇨ put in place protection programmes, including recovery and rehabilitation, to offer emergency and long-term support to all children trapped in slavery-like conditions.
⇨ ensure education is offered in ways that support the removal of children involved in the worst forms of child labour; for example, that it is accessible, flexible and affordable.
Save the Children is calling on the public to:
⇨ lobby their MPs to make the elimination of child slavery a priority.
⇨ support fair trade initiatives that protect the rights of child labourers.
25 March 2007

⇨ The above information is reprinted with kind permission from Save the Children. Visit www.savethechildren.org.uk for more information on this and other related topics.

© *Save the Children*

Child soldiers

Information from the Coalition to Stop the Use of Child Soldiers

'I would like you to give a message. Please do your best to tell the world what is happening to us, the children. So that other children don't have to pass through this violence.'

The 15-year-old girl who ended an interview to Amnesty International with this plea was forcibly abducted at night from her home by the Lord's Resistance Army (LRA), an armed opposition movement fighting the Ugandan Government. She was made to kill a boy who tried to escape. She saw another boy being hacked to death for not raising the alarm when a friend ran away. She was beaten when she dropped a water container and ran for cover under gunfire. She received 35 days of military training and was sent to fight the government army.

The use of children as soldiers has been universally condemned as abhorrent and unacceptable. Yet over the last ten years hundreds of thousands of children have fought and died in conflicts around the world.

Children involved in armed conflict are frequently killed or injured during combat or while carrying out other tasks. They are forced to engage in hazardous activities such as laying mines or explosives, as well as using weapons. Child soldiers are usually forced to live under harsh conditions with insufficient food and little or no access to healthcare. They are almost always treated brutally, subjected to beatings and humiliating treatment. Punishments for mistakes or desertion are often very severe. Girl soldiers are particularly at risk of rape, sexual harassment and abuse as well as being involved in combat and other tasks.

Some facts
⇨ The problem is most critical in Africa, where children as young as nine have been involved in armed conflicts. Children are also used as soldiers in various Asian countries and in parts of Latin America, Europe and the Middle East.

Children as young as nine have been abducted and used in combat

---

⇨ The majority of the world's child soldiers are involved in a variety of armed political groups. These include government-backed paramilitary groups, militias and self-defence units operating in many conflict zones. Others include armed groups opposed to central government rule, groups composed of ethnic religious and other minorities and clan-based or factional groups fighting governments and each other to defend territory and resources.
⇨ Most child soldiers are aged between 14 and 18. While many enlist 'voluntarily' research shows that such adolescents see few alternatives to involvement in armed conflict. Some enlist as a means of survival in war-torn regions after family, social and economic structures collapse

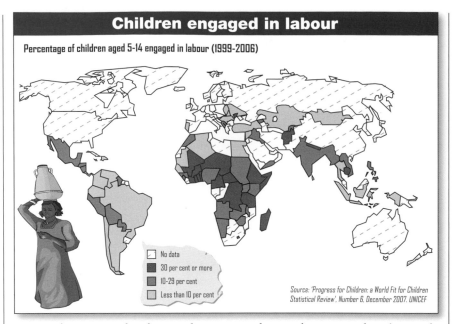

Children engaged in labour

Percentage of children aged 5-14 engaged in labour (1999-2006)

- No data
- 30 per cent or more
- 10-29 per cent
- Less than 10 per cent

Source: 'Progress for Children: a World Fit for Children Statistical Review', Number 6, December 2007. UNICEF

or after seeing family members tortured or killed by government forces or armed groups. Others join up because of poverty and lack of work or educational opportunities. Many girls have reported enlisting to escape domestic servitude, violence and sexual abuse.

⇨ Forcible abductions, sometimes of large numbers of children, continue to occur in some countries. Children as young as nine have been abducted and used in combat.

⇨ Demobilisation, disarmament and reintegration (DDR) programmes specifically aimed at child soldiers have been established in many countries, both during and after armed conflict, and have assisted former child soldiers to acquire new skills and return to their communities. However, the programmes lack funds and adequate resources. Sustained long-term investment is needed if they are to be effective.

⇨ Despite growing recognition of girls' involvement in armed conflict, girls are often deliberately or inadvertently excluded from DDR programmes. Girl soldiers are frequently subjected to rape and other forms of sexual violence as well as being involved in combat and other roles. In some cases they are stigmatised by their home communities when they return. DDR programmes should be sensitively constructed and

designed to respond to the needs of girl soldiers.

⇨ See www.childsoldiersglobal report.org for lists of countries where child soldiers were recruited and used during the four years 2004-2007.

Why children join

Children are forcibly recruited into armed groups in many conflicts but the vast majority of child soldiers are adolescents between the age of 14 and 18 who 'volunteer' to join up. However, research has shown that a number of factors may be involved in

making the decision to actually join an armed conflict and in reality many such adolescents see few alternatives to enlisting. War itself is a major determinant. Economic, social, community and family structures are frequently ravaged by armed conflict and joining the ranks of the fighters is often the only means of survival. Many youths have reported that desire to avenge the killing of relatives or other violence arising from war is an important motive.

Poverty and lack of access to educational or work opportunities are additional factors – with joining up often holding out either the promise or the reality of an income or a means of getting one. Coupled with this may be a desire for power, status or social recognition. Family and peer pressure to join up for ideological or political reasons or to honour family tradition may also be motivating factors. Girl soldiers have reported joining up to escape domestic servitude or enforced marriage or get away from domestic violence, exploitation and abuse.

⇨ The above information is reprinted with kind permission from the Coalition to Stop the Use of Child Soldiers. Visit www.child-soldiers.org for more information.

© Coalition to Stop the Use of Child Soldiers

Child trafficking – facts

Information from ECPAT UK

⇨ 2.45 million people are victims of trafficking annually, of which 50% are children (ILO, 2005).

⇨ Trafficking is worth an estimated US$ 32 billion each year (ILO, 2005).

⇨ ECPAT UK found a total of 35 child trafficking cases in 17 London boroughs in 2003. In addition, 32 out of 33 London boroughs expressed concerns about trafficked children in their care (ECPAT UK, 2004).

⇨ In 2001, West Sussex Social Services reported that 66 children had gone missing from its care since 1995. Evidence suggests they were further trafficked by the people who initially brought them into the country (ECPAT UK, 2004).

⇨ UNICEF reported there were 250 child trafficking cases in the UK between 1998 and 2003 (UNICEF UK, 2003).

⇨ The above information is reprinted with kind permission from ECPAT UK. Visit www.ecpat.org.uk for more information.

© ECPAT UK

All equal?

Information from the Children's Rights Alliance for England

By Adam Roberts, age 15

We've all grown up believing children are different. In a sense, they are: they're younger than everyone else – but they're still people, they've still got feelings, and, like adults, they still need some respect. Yet children aren't taken seriously; until they're 18, nothing they say or do really makes any difference.

I've spent the past 15 years of my life being a kid, so I know what it's like to be one. When I walk home from school, I see signs outside the shops, over and over again: '2 children at a time'; 'no bags'; even little printed notices barring you completely 'unless accompanied by an adult'. Imagine if you were a child: waiting forever for your turn, and even then, watching the adults push you away, stroll into the shop, neither knowing nor caring how long you've been there. And why? Because they're adults.

And what of those other signs? 'No bags', for example? You'd be offended, and rightly so, if someone asked you to leave your suitcase or handbag at the door. Those adults who don't have children many not realise how much a musical instrument or kit bag can cost: more than you'd even consider paying for the laptop you'd be forced to leave – unguarded – outside the shop.

I often go out to watch a film at the local cinema, as many of my friends do. The thing is, once you're over 15, you pay the same amount as an adult. Even though you can't work, at least without a special permit, you have to pay just as much as those who have a job. And you don't qualify for the Minimum Wage. It gets worse when you realise that the price of cinema tickets drops again if you're an adult and in full-time education like we are. Yes, they're studying, but so are we, and we don't get this discount. We earn little or nothing, but we pay more.

Don't think we haven't tried to stop it. There have been campaigns in the past to try and get local businesses to change their ways, but frankly, they don't care. We're children; we can't even vote. We're normal, reasonable people, and yet no one bats an eyelid whether we get any respect or not.

A few years ago the local council decided to change the catchment areas for our local schools, each of which offers different opportunities, and is therefore better suited to different people. The council launched a consultation, yet they sought the opinions of our parents, not us.

Perhaps, this year, things may start to change. CRAE recently released an extensive report on how well the Government is protecting children's rights. This June, a delegation of 12 children from around England presented the report to a UN Committee in Geneva, Switzerland, who will then take the issues further.

So what does this report – written and researched by children – actually say about children, and whether they're given the respect they deserve? In fact, quite a lot.

They raised the issue of whether children are treated fairly in the media: the sweeping generalisations and unsupported stereotypes they are faced with, which in turn lead to many other issues, especially with regard to how children are treated. They identified particular groups which respected children least, such as councillors and MPs, bus drivers, and shop assistants.

They found huge numbers of children were discriminated against racially, and that very few knew how to formally complain if adults seriously abused them. They found that only around half of children had been consulted following a divorce as to which parent they would live with, and only a minority of children had access to or knew of counselling and mental health services in their area.

Unsurprisingly, they raised the issue of whether older children – those above 16 – should be allowed to vote. Though this may not seem like an issue with much credit, there are many convincing arguments for it: for example, these children can leave home, marry, apply for a job, fight and even die for their country, and yet still not vote; they can also, crucially, pay taxes to a government they don't even have a right to vote for. For children to be properly respected – especially by MPs, identified in the report as some of the worst offenders – they need to be taken seriously.

CRAE's message to the UN is crucial for so many children, many of whom are subjected to abuses far more serious than children in my area will ever be faced with. The UN takes children seriously; the government, so far, hasn't. Politicians never grow tired of that age-old sentiment: 'children are our future'. What they fail to realise, or perhaps simply overlook, is that children are our present too. Perhaps, just for once, they'll listen.
4 July 2008

⇨ The above information is re-printed with kind permission from the Children's Rights Alliance for England. Visit www.getreadyforchange.org.uk for more information.
© Children's Rights Alliance for England

Smacking – facts, figures and arguments

Information from the Children Are Unbeatable! Alliance

The Children Are Unbeatable! Alliance campaigns for the UK to satisfy human rights obligations by modernising the law on assault to afford children the same protection as adults. The Alliance was established in 1998 and is now the broadest campaign coalition ever assembled on a children's issue, bringing together more than 400 organisations and many more individuals.

What do we want?

We simply want children to have equal protection. 'Smacking' is already banned – for all people except children.

The law still allows parents and others to justify common assault of children as 'reasonable punishment'. This defence is unjust and unsafe, and must be abolished now.

This simple reform will send a clear message that hitting children, however we dress it up, is as unacceptable and unlawful as hitting anyone else.

Giving children less protection under the law on assault is disrespectful. Children are people with human rights to physical integrity and human dignity just like the rest of us.

What the United Nations says

In October 2008, the United Nations Committee on the Rights of the Child stated in its concluding observations on the UK: 'The Committee is concerned at the failure of State party to explicitly prohibit all corporal punishment in the home and emphasises its view that the existence of any defence in cases of corporal punishment of children does not comply with the principles and provisions of the Convention, since it would suggest that some forms of corporal punishment are acceptable.'

In June 2006, the United Nations Committee on the Rights of the Child said that giving children equal protection from assault is 'an immediate and unqualified obligation' under the Convention on the Rights of the Child.

'Violence against children is a violation of their human rights, a disturbing reality of our societies. It can never be justified whether for disciplinary reasons or cultural tradition. No such thing as a "reasonable" level of violence is acceptable. Legalised violence against children in one context risks tolerance of violence against children generally.'
Louise Arbour, United Nations High Commissioner for Human Rights

What the Council of Europe says

'...Article 17 [of the European Social Charter] requires a prohibition in legislation against any form of violence against children, whether at school, in other institutions, in their home or elsewhere.'
European Committee of Social Rights 'General Observation' on corporal punishment, 2001

In July 2005, the European Committee of Social Rights found UK law in breach of human rights obligations. It concluded: '...since there is no prohibition in legislation of all corporal punishment in the home, the situation [in the UK] is not in conformity with Article 17 of the Charter'.

'For the Council of Europe, children are not mini-persons with mini-rights, mini-feelings and mini-human dignity. They are vulnerable human beings with full rights which require more, not less protection. It is therefore absolutely unacceptable that when it comes to the protection of their physical and psychological integrity, they should be worse off than adults.'
Maud de Boer-Buquicchio, Deputy Secretary General of the Council of Europe, 2005

What UK politicians say

Rt Hon Kevin Barron MP, chair of the Health Select Committee, said: 'Hitting children, even if we dress it up with cosy euphemisms like

HE... HE... HE...

...WAS JUST BEING A CHILD

"smacking", hurts emotionally and physically. Zero tolerance of domestic violence is rightly accepted as a sensible standard for modern times, and it should be equally so where the well-being of children is concerned.'

Rt Hon Lord Kinnock said: 'Our human rights obligations to respect the physical integrity and human dignity of children are clear. To fulfil those obligations properly, children must be given the protection of the law against assault which adults take for granted in a civilised society. And we should do it quickly, before the 21st century gets much older.'

Lord St John of Fawsley said: 'The case for ending the legal and social acceptance of hitting children is unanswerable. In the 21st century it is time for all of us to move on. Affording children equal protection under the law on assault seems to me a very modest, yet essential, step in the right direction.'

Annette Brooke MP, Liberal Democrat spokesperson on children and the family, said: 'As modern liberals, we often have to balance rights for different individuals and groups. On this issue, the current law has the balance all wrong. There can be no justification for the smallest and most fragile of our citizens having less protection from assault than the rest of us.'

Greg Pope MP said: 'Support for this mainstream social reform is growing all the time in Westminster. It is now time for everyone with a stake in modern progressive politics to stand up and be counted. We cannot escape our human rights obligations to give children equal protection from assault; nor should we want to.'

Elfyn Llwyd MP, Plaid Cymru parliamentary leader, said: 'I truly believe that ending the legal and social acceptability of hitting children is one of the key tests of a modern civilised society. As such, giving children equal protection from assault is essential to drive forward the necessary cultural change.'

The professional consensus

'Hitting children hurts, humiliates and harms. Health professionals say let's stop defending this violent behaviour and change the law now so that parents can move on to use more effective methods of discipline.'
Dr Cheryll Adams, Lead Professional Officer, UNITE – Community Practitioners' and Heath Visitors' Association

Professional organisations supporting the Children Are Unbeatable! Alliance include:
⇨ 4Children
⇨ Association of Educational Psychologists
⇨ Barnardo's
⇨ British Association for the Study & Prevention of Child Abuse & Neglect
⇨ British Association of Social Workers
⇨ Community Practitioners' and Health Visitors' Association
⇨ Daycare Trust
⇨ Kidscape
⇨ National Association of Probation Officers
⇨ National Childminding Association
⇨ National Children's Bureau
⇨ NSPCC
⇨ National Youth Agency
⇨ NCH
⇨ Parenting UK
⇨ Royal College of Midwives
⇨ Royal College of Paediatrics and Child Health
⇨ Save the Children UK
⇨ The Children's Society
⇨ Women's Aid Federation of England.

Most professional organisations contributing to the Government's consultation on 'reasonable punishment' (section 58 of the Children Act 2004) in 2007 criticised the current law for being unjust and called for equal protection for children.

Who else has called for equal protection?

⇨ The UK's Children's Commissioners (2006)
⇨ The independent Commission on the Family and the Wellbeing of Children (2005)
⇨ The National Assembly for Wales (2004)
⇨ The UK parliamentary Joint Committee on Human Rights (2003)
⇨ The House of Commons Health Select Committee (2003).

'Children have the same right as adults to respect for their human dignity and physical integrity and to equal protection under the law, in the home and everywhere else. There is no room for compromise...'
Joint statement by the UK Children's Commissioners, 2006

Where do children already have equal protection?

Law reform to give children equal protection from assault is accelerating fast across Europe, changing attitudes for the better and without great controversy. Nineteen countries – more than a third of the member states of the Council of Europe – now give children equal protection: Austria (1989), Bulgaria (2000), Croatia (1999), Cyprus (1994), Denmark (1997), Finland (1983), Germany (2000), Greece (2006), Hungary (2004), Iceland (2003), Italy (1996 by supreme court ruling), Latvia (1998), Netherlands (2007), Norway (1987), Portugal (2007), Romania (2004), Spain (2007), Sweden (1979) and Ukraine (2004).

Ten reasons to support equal protection

Human rights obligations
The UN Committee on the Rights of the Child has twice recommended law reform; the European Social Charter requires abolition of all corporal punishment, and the European Court of Human Rights has ruled that UK law does not provide adequate protection.
Children are being legally hit right now
Research commissioned by the Department of Health shows that most UK children are hit and around a third are hit severely (Smith and Nobes, 1997).
Support child protection professionals
All those involved in protecting children from abuse, from the NSPCC to Social Services Directors, want the law changed to provide a clear basis for child protection.
Promote positive parenting
The law as it stands undermines the work of health visitors, midwives, early years carers and many others who try to promote positive, non-violent discipline.

Cultural change

The law sets standards in every sphere of society, including family relationships. How can we expect parents to stop hitting their children if the law says it's acceptable?

Reform works

Children are afforded equal protection from assault in Germany, Sweden, Denmark, Austria and many other countries, changing attitudes and behaviour for the better.

The law is archaic

The law allowing children to be legally hit dates back to the 19th century and is out of step with the values of a modern society.

Ordinary people do not oppose change

In fact, when asked in a non-sensationalist way, the majority of people support changing the law to give children equal protection (MORI Social Affairs Institute, 2004).

It's the right thing to do

Many countries have changed their laws without having public opinion firmly on their side. They did it because it is the right thing to do for children, children's rights and child protection, and public attitudes have changed as a result.

Hitting children is wrong

...and the law should say so.

Facts

⇨ In 2004, the MORI Social Affairs Institute found that seven in ten British people (71 per cent) support a change in the law to give children equal protection from being hit in the family home.

⇨ A growing number of Christian and faith groups support equal protection for children, including the Methodist and United Reformed Churches.

⇨ The last major UK study (Smith and Nobes for the Department of Health, 2007), interviewing parents and children, found that the large majority (91 per cent) of children had been hit.

⇨ Children agree that 'smacking' is hitting. Most young children in a study (NCB and Save the Children, 1997) described a 'smack' as a hard or very hard hit.

⇨ The above information is reprinted with kind permission from the Children are Unbeatable! Alliance.

Visit www.childrenareunbeatable.org.uk for more information.

© Children are Unbeatable! Alliance

Treatment of children in the UK

UN human rights body once again condemns treatment of children in the UK

A highly critical report published today (Friday, 3 October) by the United Nations Committee on the Rights of the Child has slammed the UK Government as failing to meet international standards on the treatment of children. In a number of vital areas – from juvenile justice to the rights of disabled children, from the protection of young asylum seekers to the right of children to privacy – the Government is failing to meet its obligations under international law. As part of over 120 recommendations made to the UK Government, the UN report calls for the review and abolition of the use of anti-social behaviour orders for children and for tighter regulation of reality television programmes that feature babies and children. The UN Committee urges the Government, as a matter of priority, to prohibit corporal punishment in the family.

Carolyne Willow, National Co-ordinator of the Children's Rights Alliance for England, said: 'We now call for the Government to take immediate action to remedy breaches in the Convention on the Rights of the Child and we want the Convention brought into UK law as a matter of urgency. Given the severity and breadth of the criticisms made by the UN Committee, Ed Balls must now make a statement to the House as soon as possible after parliament resumes next week.'

The UN Committee on the Rights of the Child is an international body of 18 children's human rights experts established to monitor how well UN States Parties implement the Convention on the Rights of the Child. Every five years the UK Government is required to report to and then be examined by this UN body for its treatment of the UK's 13.1 million children. Government representatives faced detailed questioning by members of the Committee last week (nearly 200 questions); the examination was observed by NGOs, the Children's Commissioners and children and young people.

3 October 2008

⇨ The above information is reprinted with kind permission from the Children's Rights Alliance for England. Visit www.crae.org.uk for more information.

© Children's Rights Alliance for England

Smacking children is a decision for parents

By Jenny McCartney

Britain was more preoccupied last week by the news that Richard Fuld, the former head of Lehman Brothers, had reportedly been punched while exercising in his office gym, than by the age-old question of whether parents should smack their children.

And so it was that a Parliamentary amendment seeking to ban smacking outright – eclipsed by Gordon Brown's emergency statement on the financial crisis – was never even put to MPs during the debate on the Children and Young Person's Bill.

The smacking debate is both well-worn and notoriously tricky

This, I have to say, came as some relief: the smacking debate is both well-worn and notoriously tricky. The clause, however, was supported by 100 Labour MPs, and its demise was lamented by Tony Samphier of the Children Are Unbeatable! Alliance, who rather dramatically said that ministers should now be conscience-stricken over the 'hurt that every child feels while being legally assaulted'.

For once, however, I find myself in agreement with Beverley Hughes, the Children's Minister, who recently wrote that 'we do not encourage or condone smacking... neither do we support a ban which would make smacking a crime'.

That, she said, would mean that criminal charges could be brought against a mother who gave her child a mild smack on the hand for refusing to put back sweets grabbed at the supermarket checkout.

The trouble with opposing, however mildly, something like the Children Are Unbeatable! Alliance is that it makes one sound like some bewhiskered lunatic who staunchly believes that children should be beatable. The virulent anti-smacking campaigners always talk about 'hitting' and 'assaulting' children, rather than smacking, but a sharp tap on the hand of a child who is about to run across a busy road, for example, would not be my definition of assault.

I understand the arguments. I am not a smacker myself, partly because the difference in size between me and my two-and-a-half-year-old son would make such an action feel vaguely grotesque. Nor do I believe that – in the midst of a tantrum, say – it would do more than goad him to greater heights of confused rage. But I know loving parents who smack their children lightly as a means of disciplining them *in extremis*, and the idea of them being hauled off for police questioning on the say-so of some eagle-eyed stranger is deeply disturbing in itself.

We are not talking here about parents who hit their children with serious force, or to the point of leaving a mark or a weal. That is quite a different matter, and to pretend that it is part and parcel of the same thing is to defy common sense.

There is, perhaps, no issue that so clearly marks the difference in attitudes between the older and younger generations as that of physical punishment. Many adults from the generations that grew up before and immediately after the Second World War were deeply conflicted on the matter: they saw it almost as a duty by which they must shape the wilful nature of the child, and yet they felt ashamed at their own ugly loss of control in enacting it.

The result was a form of parenting that Philip Larkin memorably described as 'soppy stern', and the responses of children to it were equally complex. The broadcaster Richard Madeley has recently written, with moving insight, of the painful thrashings that he suffered at the hands of his father, a man who was also highly affectionate. His father eventually stopped the beatings, with a sincere expression of contrition, and the pair remained close: the child found it in him to forgive the man.

My late grandfather was caned, aged eight, by a young female teacher for falling asleep at his school desk: he was woken by the searing pain of the blow. My father recalls crying uncontrollably – with laughter, at an illicit joke – as the headmaster belaboured him with the cane.

Neither man bore any particular grudge, but I will never forget the haunting story of a London taxi driver who told me how he was regularly beaten, in secret, by a particularly sadistic master at his school. He said nothing until he discovered that the master was starting on his little sister, whereupon he entered the room and attacked the master with his own richly overused cane.

Such brutal practices have rightly been outlawed, but the orthodoxy has swung to the opposite extreme. Authority figures such as teachers and policemen are now effectively forbidden from making any decisive physical response to unruly teenagers.

Hulking boys of 14 and 15, who suffer no such inhibitions when it comes to shoving around their younger or weaker schoolmates, chant the Childline number if a teacher lays a restraining hand on them. A policeman who picked a cheeky teenager up and briefly placed him in a bin in 2005, to the loud laughter of the boy's friend, was given a written warning and the boy received £4,000 in compensation.

Out-of-control adolescents have got the message that not only are they unbeatable, they are also untouchable. The consequences for the rest of society are frequently unthinkable.

12 October 2008

⇨ The ideas behind human rights have been present throughout history in many different societies and civilisations. However, the modern concept of human rights emerged in the twentieth century as a response to the events of the Second World War, particularly the mass crimes committed during the Holocaust. (page 1)

⇨ In the UK today, a number of fundamental individual freedoms are protected by the Human Rights Act 1998. This requires all UK law to comply with the European Convention on Human Rights of 1950 (and its First and Sixth Protocols), makes the Convention enforceable in UK courts, and requires the judiciary to interpret domestic law so as to comply with the Convention. Appeals against the rulings of UK courts can still be taken to the European Court of Human Rights, as they could be prior to the Act. (page 4)

⇨ 74% of men and 76% of women polled supported the statement 'Britain should have, and use, the right to imprison foreign terrorist suspects for as long as the authorities judge necessary, unless they choose to return to their home country'. (page 7)

⇨ 60% of men surveyed agreed with the statement 'Britain should have, and use, the right to deport foreigners suspected by the intelligence services, even if there is not enough courtroom evidence to bring them to trial, and they might be sent to countries where they could be tortured'. This compared with 50% of women who supported the statement. (page 7)

⇨ Article 1 of the Universal Declaration of Human Rights states that 'All human beings are born free and equal in dignity and rights. They are endowed with reason and conscience and should act towards one another in a spirit of brotherhood'. (page 8)

⇨ Amnesty International documented cases of torture and other cruel, inhuman or degrading treatment in more than 81 countries in 2007. (page 14)

⇨ The Human Rights Act may be used by every person resident in England or Wales regardless of whether or not they are a British citizen or a foreign national, a child or an adult, a prisoner or a member of the public. It can even be used by companies or organisations. (page 15)

⇨ The Human Rights Act doesn't protect an endless catalogue of rights. Indeed, it only protects 15 well-established fundamental rights and freedoms, like the right to life and free speech. Many other democracies protect a far broader range of rights. Our human rights laws do not, for example, create general rights to a home,

to live in the UK or to receive benefits. (page 17)

⇨ 56% of people surveyed agreed that 'people only talk about their human rights when they're trying to get something they're not entitled to'. (page 19)

⇨ An estimated 126 million children work in the worst forms of child labour – one in 12 of the world's 5- to 17-year-olds. (page 20)

⇨ Some UK-based companies, knowingly or not, rely on people working in slavery to produce goods that they sell: complex sub-contracting and supply chains, managed by agents elsewhere, often obscure this involvement. (page 21)

⇨ A YouGov poll conducted on behalf of think-tank MigrationWatch showed that, when asked if the UK should renounce its membership of the Convention in order to have greater powers to deal with suspected and convicted terrorists, 61% agreed. Just 26% supported the proposition that Britain should remain a member of the Human Rights Convention, and not reduce human rights in response to the terrorist threat. (page 24)

⇨ Eighteen countries have changed the law to stop parents hitting their children (the date in brackets is when the law was changed) – Sweden (1979), Finland (1983), Norway (1987), Austria (1989), Cyprus (1994), Denmark (1997), Latvia (1998), Croatia (1999), Germany (2000), Bulgaria (2000), Israel (2000), Iceland (2003), Romania (2004), Ukraine (2004), Hungary (2005), Greece (2006), the Netherlands (2007) and New Zealand (2007). (page 30)

⇨ Child labourers are not confined to poor countries. In the industrial countries, around 2.5 million children aged 5-14 are economically active, or around 2% of the total child population. In countries with transition economies, including former socialist countries, 2.4 million children aged 5-14, or around 4% of the total child population, are economically active. (page 31)

⇨ At any one time across the world, around 1.8 million children are being abused through prostitution, child pornography and sex tourism. (page 32)

⇨ 2.45 million people are victims of trafficking annually, of which 50% are children (ILO, 2005). (page 34)

⇨ In 2004, the MORI Social Affairs Institute found that seven in ten British people (71 per cent) support a change in the law to give children equal protection from being hit in the family home. (page 38)

GLOSSARY

Child labour

Up to 352 million children worldwide were classed as 'economically active' in 2002, 246 million of whom were classed as 'child labourers' by the International Labour Organisation (16% of the world's children). Many will be doing work which is physically or mentally hazardous to them and which interferes with their education or social development.

European Convention on Human Rights

The Convention was adopted by the Council of Europe in 1950 to enshrine the articles of the Universal Declaration of Human Rights. The UK signed up to the Convention in 1951.

Human rights

The basic rights all human beings are entitled to, regardless of who they are, where they live or what they do. Concepts of human rights have been present throughout history, but our modern understanding of the term emerged as a response to the horrific events of the Holocaust.

The Human Rights Act

The Human Rights Act is a written law (statute) passed in 1998 which is in force in England and Wales. The human rights that are contained within this law are based on the articles of the European Convention on Human Rights.

Slavery

A slave is someone who is denied their freedom, forced to work without pay and considered to be literally someone else's property. Although slavery is officially banned internationally, there are an estimated 27 million slaves worldwide. Article 4 of the Universal Declaration of Human Rights states that 'No one shall be held in slavery or servitude; slavery and the slave trade shall be prohibited in all their forms.'

Torture

Intentionally causing a person physical or mental pain or suffering in order to obtain information or force them to make a confession. Under Article 5 of the Universal Declaration of Human Rights, 'No one shall be subjected to torture or to cruel, inhuman or degrading treatment or punishment.' The subject of torture, and whether it might be considered a necessary evil in the war against terror, has recently been the subject of controversy.

Trafficking

The transport and/or trade of people from one area to another, usually for the purpose of forcing them into labour or prostitution. According to 2005 statistics from the International Labour Organisation, 2.45 million people are victims of trafficking annually, of which 50% are children.

United Nations Convention on the Rights of the Child (UNCRC)

An international human rights treaty that protects the rights of all children and young people under 18. The UK signed the convention on 19 April 1990, ratified it on 16 December 1991 and it came into force in the UK on 15 January 1992. When a country ratifies the convention it agrees to do everything it can to implement it. Every country in the world has signed the convention except the USA and Somalia.

Universal Declaration of Human Rights

The first international, secular agreement on what were formerly called 'the rights of man', which arose from the desire of the worlds governments to prevent the recurrence of the atrocities of the Second World War by setting out a shared bill of rights for all peoples and all nations. The text is non-binding, but it retains its force as the primary authority on human rights, and has been supported by the UN's ongoing work to encourage its incorporation into domestic laws.

INDEX

Additional Resources

Other Issues titles

If you are interested in researching further some of the issues raised in *Our Human Rights*, you may like to read the following titles in the **Issues** series:

- ⇨ Vol. 168 *Privacy and Surveillance* (ISBN 978 1 86168 472 1)
- ⇨ Vol. 159 *An Ageing Population* (ISBN 978 1 86168 452 3)
- ⇨ Vol. 154 *The Gender Gap* (ISBN 978 1 86168 441 7)
- ⇨ Vol. 153 *Sexual Orientation and Society* (ISBN 978 1 86168 440 0)
- ⇨ Vol. 152 *Euthanasia and the Right to Die* (ISBN 978 1 86168 439 4)
- ⇨ Vol. 150 *Migration and Population* (ISBN 978 1 86168 423 3)
- ⇨ Vol. 148 *Religious Beliefs* (ISBN 978 1 86168 421 9)
- ⇨ Vol. 147 *The Terrorism Problem* (ISBN 978 1 86168 420 2)
- ⇨ Vol. 135 *Coping with Disability* (ISBN 978 1 86168 387 8)
- ⇨ Vol. 131 *Citizenship and National Identity* (ISBN 978 1 86168 377 9)
- ⇨ Vol. 126 *The Abortion Debate* (ISBN 978 1 86168 365 6)
- ⇨ Vol. 121 *The Censorship Debate* (ISBN 978 1 86168 354 0)
- ⇨ Vol. 115 *Racial Discrimination* (ISBN 978 1 86168 348 9)
- ⇨ Vol. 99 *Exploited Children* (ISBN 978 1 86168 313 7)
- ⇨ Vol. 89 *Refugees* (ISBN 978 1 86168 290 1)

For more information about these titles, visit our website at www.independence.co.uk/publicationslist

Useful organisations

You may find the websites of the following organisations useful for further research:

- ⇨ **Amnesty International:** www.amnesty.org
- ⇨ **British Institute of Human Rights:** www.bihr.org.uk
- ⇨ **Children are Unbeatable! Alliance:** www.childrenareunbeatable.org.uk
- ⇨ **Children's Rights Alliance for England:** www.getreadyforchange.org.uk
- ⇨ **Coalition to Stop the Use of Child Soldiers:** www.child-soldiers.org
- ⇨ **Commission for Equality and Human Rights:** www.equalityhumanrights.com
- ⇨ **ECPAT UK:** www.ecpat.org.uk
- ⇨ **Joseph Rowntree Foundation:** www.jrf.org.uk
- ⇨ **Liberty:** www.liberty-human-rights.org.uk
- ⇨ **Medical Foundation for the Care of Victims of Torture:** www.torturecare.org.uk
- ⇨ **Migration Watch:** www.migrationwatch.org.uk
- ⇨ **New Internationalist:** www.newint.org
- ⇨ **Politics.co.uk:** www.politics.co.uk
- ⇨ **Save the Children:** www.savethechildren.org.uk
- ⇨ **UNICEF:** www.unicef.org.uk
- ⇨ **United Nations:** www.un.org

ACKNOWLEDGEMENTS

The publisher is grateful for permission to reproduce the following material.

While every care has been taken to trace and acknowledge copyright, the publisher tenders its apology for any accidental infringement or where copyright has proved untraceable. The publisher would be pleased to come to a suitable arrangement in any such case with the rightful owner.

Chapter One: Human Rights

Introducing human rights, © British Institute of Human Rights, *Human rights and politics*, © Adfero, *Human rights timeline*, © British Institute of Human Rights, *The Universal Declaration of Human Rights*, © Public domain, *Tears and smiles in the fight for justice*, © Guardian Newspapers Limited, *Amnesty International Report 2008*, © Amnesty International, *Inside the Human Rights Act*, © Liberty, *Human Rights Act is a law for ne'er-do-wells*, © Telegraph Group Limited, *Mythbuster: the Human Rights Act*, © Liberty, *Public attitudes to human rights*, © Commission for Equality and Human Rights, *Facts about modern slavery*, © Reuters, *Slavery in modern Britain*, © Joseph Rowntree Foundation, *Trafficking cases*, © Amnesty International, *Human rights in a time of terror*, © New Internationalist, *Public support for terror measures*, © Migration Watch, *Torture: myths and facts*, © Medical Foundation for the Care of Victims of Torture.

Chapter Two: Young People's Rights

Children's rights, © UNICEF, *Children's rights – the facts*, © Children's Rights Alliance for England, *Child labour*, © UNICEF, *Widespread forms of child slavery*, © Save the Children, *Child soldiers*, © Coalition to Stop the Use of Child Soldiers, *Child trafficking – facts*, © ECPAT UK, *All equal?*, © Children's Rights Alliance for England, *Smacking – facts, figures and arguments*, © Children are Unbeatable! Alliance, *Treatment of children in the UK*, © Children's Rights Alliance for England, *Smacking children is a decision for parents*, © Telegraph Group Limited.

Photographs

Flickr: pages 11 (Alex Steffler); 19 (Trevor Stone); 26 (takomabibelot); 35 (Cory Doctorow); 38 (hydra arts).
Stock Xchng: pages 9 (Gary Cowles); 27 (Val Kerry); 31 (Supreet Vaid); 32 (Sophie).
Wikimedia Commons: page 17 (Trialsanderrors).

Illustrations

Pages 1, 12, 23: Angelo Madrid; pages 3, 10, 36: Simon Kneebone; pages 5, 16, 33: Don Hatcher; pages 8, 15: Bev Aisbett.

Research and additional editorial by Claire Owen, on behalf of Independence Educational Publishers.

And with thanks to the team: Mary Chapman, Sandra Dennis, Claire Owen and Jan Sunderland.

Lisa Firth
Cambridge
January, 2009